Praise for
Freedom from **Fat**

Do you want to be more successful?
Read this book!
Do you want to help others be more successful?
Give them this book!
Mark Matteson cracks the success code in an easy-to-read, fun story, with lessons for all of us.

> David Heimer
> Chief Operating Officer,
> Service Nation, Inc.

A blueprint for success in life!

> Patrick Snow
> Author, Speaker

Ever wonder why some people seem to succeed at everything they do in life? This book explains it perfectly. It provides a blueprint for success!

> Clay Moyle
> Author

Bestselling author Mark Matteson's *Freedom from Fat* will grab you by the lapels and transform your wishes into the will to get the waistline and health you desire. Along the way, you will have the good fortune of being entertained by Mark's talented storytelling.

> Janette Turner
> Author, Coach

Reading Mark's latest book will remind you of the joy of friendship—truly great friendship—and how you can be motivated toward most any goal with enough love, passion, wisdom, and reasons. A wonderful read that will keep you smiling and alert. Be ready for changes!

Adams Hudson, Hudson, Ink Corp.
Author, Speaker, Consultant

I could not put it down. Mark has a knack for saying the right thing at the right time. The concepts that he writes about are timeless and applicable to all parts of your life and *Freedom from Fat* is great example of that. Friendship, work ethic, goal setting and all the other great messages that are always a part of his work are very much a part of this story. Ben and Charlie inspired me. They'll inspire you.

Sam Mullins
Contractor,
Nashville, Tennessee

This Book is a godsend.

Lester Wooldridge
Wooldridge Heating and Air,
Lynchburg, Virginia

Mark drives home the learning like no other author I know. His storytelling ability allows the reader to grasp the concept in relatable scenarios they can compare to their own lives. Another winner for Mark!

Roberta Aronoff
Executive Director,
Telecommunications Risk Management Association

When you are a career sales professional, you continually learn and work to get better. Mark Matteson helps the journey with time proven wisdom presented in a witty and enjoyable format. A must read!!

John Zilla
Comfort Systems USA,
Williamsburg, Virginia

As always, Mark reaches into your mind and heart with his unique way of asking questions, and gently guides the reader through subtle insights to enrichment. Nicely done, Mark; you are making a difference.

Tom Piscitelli
Author, Speaker

With all of the latest and greatest books on personal growth and positive life change, Mark finally brought me back to the simple truths I thought I had learned years ago. These are foundational principles upon which success and significance are built, and Mark drives these home through a highly engaging and creative tale. Excellent read!

Mike Greene,
Author,
60 Second Time Out and 60 Second Leadership

Mark Matteson's new book reminds us that as we develop our mental, emotional, and spiritual selves we must remember that our body is the vessel of our intellect and cannot be ignored. *Freedom from Fat* will change your life.

Jim Donovan
Author, *Take Charge of Your Destiny*

FREEDOM FROM FAT

A Tale of
Two Brothers

MARK MATTESON

Ugly Dog Publishing
206-697-0454
www.SparkingSuccess.net

ISBN: 978-0-692-92607-9

Dedication

This book is dedicated to my father, Robert D. Matteson. He was committed to doing something to stay fit and eat right every day. At age sixty-five he weighed the same as he did in college. Thanks Dad...I miss you every day.

"It was the best of times, it was the worst of times, it was the age of wisdom, it was the age of foolishness, it was the epoch of belief, it was the epoch of incredulity, it was the season of Light, it was the season of Darkness, it was the spring of hope, it was the winter of despair..."

Charles Dickens, *A Tale of Two Cities*

"...the way to wealth, if you desire it, is as plain as the way to market. It depends chiefly on two words, industry and frugality; that is, waste neither time nor money, but make the best of both. Without industry and frugality, nothing will do, and with them everything."

Benjamin Franklin, *The Way to Wealth*

"The things that happen in this world. It's a wonder God allows it."

Frank Darabont, screenwriter, *The Green Mile*
Based on the novel by Stephen King

"Americans are addicted, especially to food. They are fatally attracted to the slow death of fast food."

George Carlin, Writer, Comedian, Philosopher

Table of Contents

-Part Two-
Forward

-Part Three-
Upward

-PART ONE-
Backward

CHAPTER ONE

Whatever...

Let me tell you a story...

It's been fifty years since all this transpired, so the what should be accurate, the when however just might be a little out of focus.

One thing is clear: It was 1966, the year of Ben Franklin Jones.

There was a gentle tapping on the door, an uncertain knock, the kind a young child makes when he is not sure who will open it. A tall attractive woman, early thirties, with long auburn hair spilling gently around her shoulders, answered. "May I help you young man?"

The boy, lanky, with a charming smile and dishwater blond hair, looking like he just got out of bed said, "Do you have any children?"

Smiling as only mothers can, she replied, "Why yes, we have three. Our youngest, Benji, is about your age. He's seven."

The boy was a little more at ease now, his confidence growing. "I'll be eight next week," young Charlie said. "Can your son play?" Their conversation was brief; it lasted less than a minute.

A week later, Charlie proudly popped a 50-yard wheelie on his Schwinn Stingray. He had attached a tall, chrome "sissy bar" in back and replaced the rear balloon tire with a treadless "slick" enabling him to burn a patch of rubber on the pavement and fishtail to a stop.

One of the bike's most attractive features had little to do with its looks. On this bike, you could pop a wheelie by pulling hard on the high handlebars and riding only on the rear tire. This bike gave teens an outlaw image and helped them get comfortable with fear.

Benji, on the other hand, rode a twenty-inch Huffy Penguin. He earned the money, all $49, mowing lawns. If you asked him about his bike he would reel off the description from memory:

"The Huffy Penguin is available only in black, with the frame being a standard Huffy 20-inch cantilever design (with no fenders installed). The rear wheel has a heavy-duty single- speed with a coaster brake and chrome rim. The rear tire is a knobby-tread 20x2.125 black-wall. The front wheel is a 28-spoke middleweight with a chrome rim, and a black-wall 20x 1.75 tire. The seat is a white "Solo Polo" model with a chromed square-topped support bar in the rear. Handlebars are standard "Wald" high-riser type with white handgrips. Huffy Penguins also sport front-caliper hand brakes, and a chain-guard with the bike's name on it."

He was smart like that. Remembering things no one else ever would for their age. It was something he would do his whole life.

Benji chose this particular bike because he felt the Schwinn Stingray was for show-offs. He was deep in thought about the specs of his new bike, when some idiot came around the corner and smashed into him, knocking both of them off their bikes. As they shook off the shock of the collision, Charlie looked up at Benji. "You! What is the matter with you, man?" Benji asked. "Why don't you look where you're going?"

"Sorry. Are you okay?" Charlie asked, with the resilient forgiveness of childhood.

"Whatever..." is all Benji said.

"Look at that," said Charlie, pointing at a bird that had perched on Benji's handlebars. Charlie recognized it from the *State Symbols of Washington* poster that hung in his classroom. "It's a goldfinch, the state bird."

"Isn't that weird?" Benji replied.

"Yeah," said Charlie. Benji's bike was bright yellow with black stripes. The bird and the bike were a match. And then, just like that, it was gone.

And from that day on the two were inseparable. It's said that opposites attract. That was certainly true for Charlie and Benji. Charlie was outgoing; Ben was an introvert. Charlie loved people; Ben loved things. Charlie had a great sense of humor. Once, in 3rd grade, he made Ben laugh so hard at lunch that milk came out of his nose. That was talked about for years.

Charles Dickens Smith and Benjamin Franklin Jones had more in common than famous middle names. They had a passion for games, all kinds of games. "Flyers up," "Hide and Go Seek," "Kick the Can," and of course, "Monopoly." They would play that game for hours.

"I'm gonna be rich and famous one day," Charlie would say to Ben after he beat him in Monopoly. "Whatever..." is all Ben would ever say. Charlie was an optimist; Ben was practical, logical, and objective. He often came across as a pessimist, but he clearly wasn't.

As the years went by, the two became best friends. "Two peas in a pod," the teachers would say. They were always together at recess and they walked to school together every morning. They lived just two houses away from each other in Forest Glen, a modest neighborhood of mid-century tract houses. It was the quietest place on earth, especially at night. Birds, robins mostly, chirped you to sleep in the evenings. It was a great place for kids; it seemed like every house had at least two. It never took long to get a game of baseball going. Charlie would walk up and down the street and yell, "We got a game going! Who's in?" Charlie was like that. Fearless. Brave. Fun to be around. Ben would always be by his side, deep in thought, planning who he was going to pick so his team would win.

By the time they were twelve years old, they were on "First String," a nickname for the top level of Little League baseball, and man did they have a great team. Charlie pitched, Benji caught. Benji was the leadoff hitter and Charlie batted cleanup. In 1970 they won the Mid-City Championship and lost in the state finals 2-1. Tom Kelly was their coach and he was proud of their run. "What are you two boys doing this winter?" he asked.

"Whatever..." Benji replied.

Charlie smiled and said, "There is a reason you asked, Coach."

Ben bristled. "Why does he talk to adults that way?" he wondered to himself. "It's embarrassing and disrespectful."

Coach Kelly laughed aloud at Charlie's gumption. "Well Chuck," he replied with mock annoyance, "I have a basketball team and I want both of you to turn out. What do you say?"

Charlie paused, looked at Benji, and said, "You bet. Why not?" He rapped Benji on his shoulder. "He will too!"

Benji sneered at his best friend. "Whatever..." was all he said.

That is how their basketball careers began...

As good as they were in baseball, basketball was something special. It was fast-paced; if you made a mistake there was no time to grieve. (If you made a mistake in baseball, you had the rest of the game to think about it.) "Next play!" Coach Kelly would call out whenever a turnover happened.

Coach Kelly was a great coach. At the end of every game, he would ask the team two questions:

1) **What did we do well today?**

2) **What could we improve?**

The boys would chime in, always encouraged to share their views on what had happened. Ben loved that. It was a positive habit. Coach understood that *first you form habits, then they form you. Good habits are hard to form but easy to live with. Bad habits are easy to form and hard to live with.*

He would make certain the boys understood how important the mental side of the sport was, saying things like, "Okay, you got a guy on first and third and there is one out, the ball is hit to the shortstop, what do you do?" Hands would go up. Ben's hand was always first. Coach would let the boys talk, always saying things like, "Good, Ben. A great insight!" He was rewarding the things he wanted repeated, a strategy that Ben would use much later in life and business.

Coach would tell a story and then paraphrase the lesson by saying, *"In a Nutshell..."* In explaining what was important in basketball and why they focused on certain fundamentals over and over again, he would say, "In a Nutshell, there are three things that win basketball games:

1) **Defense**

2) **Free throws**

3) **Rebounds**"

Coach Kelly's basketball teams won 90% of their games, oftentimes at the free-throw line in the last minute. Benji was a great ball-handler and shot 92% from the line. Many a game he would hit the one-and-one free throw with seconds to go to ice the game. And if it wasn't Benji winning the game, it was Charlie hitting four or five jumpers in a row to extend an already large lead. They were the Dynamic Duo. They truly complimented each other on the court.

What Charlie liked most about hoops was that there was no limit on how good you could get. He would dribble his ball to school. He shot a hundred free throws a day. He read *Sports Illustrated* in the library. The bookmobile would come around in the summer and Charlie read every book on basketball he could get his hands on. He was especially enamored of Clair Bee who wrote sports novels with titles like *Comeback Cagers* and *Backcourt Ace*, but *Buzzer Basket* was

Charlie's favorite. He read it ten times. Basketball had become Charlie's Magnificent Obsession.

Charlie practiced two hours a day. He would drag Ben to the junior high to play against older kids twice a week. Charlie knew where every open gym was, what time it opened and closed, who would be there, which kids to pick for his team so they would win. Ben would play great defense, set screens, rebound, hit the open man. He was very unselfish. Charlie, on the other hand, loved to shoot; he always took the shot to win the game. More often than not, he would drain it. He was fearless on and off the court. After a game, Charlie would chat with the other kids, learn about their interests, laugh, tell a joke while Benji sat by himself, thinking about the game he just played and how he could improve. He was a thinker.

And that is how things went for the next six years. They played basketball every day until baseball season rolled around. Charlie had every kid's phone number memorized and would call them up and say, "Hey, we're going to the church to play from three to five today. Who can you bring with you that can play?" Once he knew there would be at least eight kids he would turn to Ben and say, "Grab your shoes and bike. Meet you out front of my house in ten minutes." Ben would mumble "Whatever..." He pretended that Charlie annoyed him but really, he loved playing ball with him. They had a magic chemistry on and off the court. They would finish each other's sentences. They would do a pick-and-roll and a give-and-go that no one could stop. This unspoken bond, of knowing just when the other guy was going to get open, where he would be; it was magical. Their play on the court only strengthened their friendship off the court.

Eventually, Charlie knew that when Ben said "Whatever..." it really meant, "I love you brother. I can't wait."

In a Nutshell

There are three things that win basketball games:

1) *Defense*

2) *Free throws*

3) *Rebounds*

"First you form habits, then they form you. Good habits are hard to form but easy to live with. Bad habits are easy to form and hard to live with."

1) *What did we do well today?*

2) *What could we improve?*

"Next Play!"

"Whatever..."

CHAPTER TWO

Teamwork

The first day of basketball camp was an awful lot like boot camp. Ed Pepple, the camp director, was a former Marine and he acted like one. He preached the gospel of Teamwork. The first evening, Coach Pepple delivered an inspirational speech that shook Charlie and Ben to their core. "Gentlemen, Basketball is life." He held up a flat, orange, uninflated basketball and asked, "What is this?" A sarcastic inner-city kid quipped, "A ball with no air!" Everyone laughed. "Correct," coach said. "It's also a metaphor. It represents the day you no longer play basketball. For some of you that may be in a year or two; for others, it may be twenty years from now. One day, your playing career will end. What you will really learn in this camp is about how to be successful in life. Basketball is life." He proceeded to read from a school-boy's notebook:

The 7 Habits of Teamwork

1) **Altruism** - Altruism is another word for unselfishness. It's the principle or practice of concern for the welfare of others. It's being "Other-Centered" in all things. How we talk to one another, helping a teammate up, giving up a good shot for a better one. It's that extra-pass philosophy. To me, teamwork is the beauty of our sport, where you have five acting as one. You become selfless. Vince Lombardi said, "Teamwork is what the Green Bay Packers were all

about. They didn't do it for individual glory. They did it because they loved one another."

2) **Industry** - Industry is hard work. Period. It's dedication to the work. It's loving the grind. Practicing your shot, running sprints, doing bench jumps to improve your vertical leap, doing pushups and sit-ups. It's choosing to do what is hard when you have easier options. It's going to the gym when your friends want you to go to a keg party. It's what you do when no one is looking. After working on your shot for two hours and wanting to quit, but shooting for another thirty minutes anyway. It's showing up early and staying later than anyone else you know.

3) **Attitude** - Attitude is a perspective, an outlook, it's being teachable. Humble. Positive. Kind. Attitude will make or break a team. It's what helps form a positive chemistry, an esprit de corps. It's the difference between winning a close game and losing it. It's saying "Yes coach, got it!" instead of "But Coach..." Birds of a feather flock together. A winning attitude is a choice and a habit; sadly, so is a losing attitude. An attitude of optimism, that is, a positive expectation combined with gratitude, is a winning combination. It will take you to the top. You choose yours every day.

4) **Study** - Having a high basketball IQ is a choice. How focused are you? How much film will you watch? To study an opponent's strengths and creating a plan to take those strengths away, like forcing a right-handed point guard to dribble with his left hand. It's letting a strong forward who is great at driving to the hoop shoot from outside. It's having your hands up on every possession. It's knowing who to foul in the closing minutes of the game, their worst free-throw shooter. The smart take from the strong every time!

5) **Goal Achievement** - It's vital that you set and achieve goals both individually and as a team. Are you the best defender on your team? What if you set a goal to shoot 85% from the free-throw line? First we work on goals, then they work on us. We become what we think about. The greatest reason to set goals is who we must become in order to achieve them! Set your goals high and don't stop until you achieve them. Setting exciting goals is the first step in turning the invisible into the visible.

6) **Good-Finding** - Are you a Good-Finder or a Fault-Finder? Are you lifting your teammates up or dragging them down? An anchor or a speedboat? Praise pays. Believing in others and telling them so in the heat of the moment can change the course of a game. "That's okay, you'll hit the next one! Shake it off! Next play!" "You got this!" It's not crying when you lose or crowing when you win. It's having class. It's giving the credit away in a win, assuming blame in a loss.

7) **Loyalty** - Love is friendship that has caught fire. It is quiet understanding, mutual confidence, sharing and forgiving. It is loyalty through good and bad times. It settles for less than perfection and makes allowances for human weaknesses. It's stepping up and stepping in.

Coach Pepple ended his talk by saying, "Basketball is life. Play it as well as you can. One day, it WILL be over. Now let's have a great week, boys!"

When he finished you could hear a pin drop. It wasn't just the content, it was the passion with which it was delivered. He lived this philosophy; he was sincere, authentic, real. After ten seconds of silence there was thunderous applause. It was like a great sermon delivered by a gifted pastor. It was very spiritual, though at the time, I didn't understand it that way. Charlie said to Ben, "He makes me want to be a better player!"

"Yeah," Ben said, "me too..."

Camp brought Ben and me closer. It helped forge what would be a lifelong friendship. Charlie never saw Ben work harder or be more committed to what he was learning. Not once did I hear Ben say, "Whatever..."

Neither of the boys was poor by any means, but they never had much. Things were tight in their homes. They never went hungry, but seconds were rare. That first day at camp, the Dynamic Duo ate massive amounts of great food, not just seconds, but thirds. One morning, Ben dared Charlie to eat twenty pancakes. He ate twenty-one! Ben had to make Charlie's bed for a week.

Twenty years later, Charlie heard Rod Stewart's *When We Were the New Boys* on the radio. It inspired him to write, "I wondered why those memories are such a treasure. Was it basketball? Was it being away from home for the first time? No. It was just because we were young. Youth is wasted on the young. Otis Redding sang, 'You don't miss your water until your well runs dry.' How true. When we are young, we think the present will last forever. The reality is, youth is frost on a windshield. I wouldn't trade all the tea in China for those times. We WERE the new boys!"

In a Nutshell

"Basketball is life."

"Show up early and stay late..."

"Yes coach, got it!"

"Teamwork is the beauty of our sport, where you have five acting as one. You become selfless."

"Loyalty is stepping up and stepping in."

"That's okay. You'll hit the next one!"

"We would never grow old, when we were the new boys."

CHAPTER THREE

First You Work on Goals...

Charlie's father saw the change in his son. He pulled him aside one Sunday after breakfast to tell him a story.

"In my eighth-grade year, I turned out for basketball. I had played one season of hoops the year before on the suggestion of my Little League baseball coach. It was a decision that would alter my life forever. When the roster was posted, my name wasn't on it. It was a rite of passage, a defining moment in my life. When you get hit with that kind of adversity at such a tender age, one of two things happen: you shrink or you grow. I got mad. I was on a mission to prove Coach Wilson wrong. I would show him.

"The following week, I approached the best player I knew, Kenny Christensen. He was an eighth-grader on the ninth-grade team scoring twenty points per game. He had more moves than a can of worms. His shot was picture perfect. He had supreme confidence. In short, he had what I wanted. I asked him, 'How did you get so good?' He looked me right in the eye and said, 'I shoot two hours a day and I attend Bob Houbreg's Basketball Camp.' The next day he brought me a brochure. Camp Casey, *July*. *$110.* I informed my parents I was going to this camp. My father smiled and said, 'You earn half, I'll pay the other half.' He saw the gleam in my eye, the fire in my belly.

"The following weekend, he nailed a hoop to the shed and gave me an old leather basketball and said, 'Show me how hard you are willing to work.' Over the next six months I wore out the grass and the net. I shot two hours a day, even in the rain. That next summer he called a friend and they built a proper concrete court and a ten-foot hoop. I continued to shoot two hours every day with game-like intensity, and that summer I attended camp. They taught me new ways to practice, and I got valuable game experience and inspiration.

"The next year my name was on the roster. Number twelve. Goal achieved.

"I attended two weeks of camp the next year. The following summer I reffed games to pay for my three weeks of camp. By my junior year, at age sixteen, I was the starting center on the varsity. Letters from colleges arrived like snowflakes from the sky. I have been setting goals ever since.

"As I reflect back upon that time, analyzing what I did OFF the court, some insights bubble to the surface. In hindsight, basketball had become my 'Magnificent Obsession.' What else did I do besides practice two hours a day?

"I read every book on basketball I could find.

"I read magazine articles in *The Sporting News* and *Sports Illustrated* looking for ideas and insights to propel me forward.

"I found open gyms five nights a week.

"I played *up* against older kids, mentors and models, every chance I got.

"I watched what little basketball was on TV.

"I attended every game I could, studying the best players of the time.

"I made friends with the school janitor and got keys to the gym.

"I shot *after* practice, sometimes until ten at night.

"I wrote goals specific to basketball—points, rebounds, FT percent, etc.—onto index cards and affirmed them five times a day.

"I *visualized* the perfect game in my imagination over and over again until one day, it happened.

"No one had to tell me to do all these things. It was a want-to not a have-to. My skills improved with each passing season. I was a sponge. I lived and slept basketball.

"Now, Charlie, a few questions for you...

"What is your number-one goal?

"How much do you want it?

"Why do you want it?

"By when?

"The right kind of goals do not include the how. Forget the how. Trust the process. The how will come if you affirm your number-one goal long enough. Affirm with passionate, positive emotion over and over again. Have faith. Persist.

"A friend of mine, a famous speaker, shared a story with me one day...

Around my fifth year as a speaker, my wife asked me why I wasn't doing Keynotes and Seminars in Hawaii or Arizona. I shrugged my shoulders and replied, "Beats me. What's wrong with New York, Boston, Philadelphia and Minneapolis in January?" "Just wondering," she said. The next day, I wrote in my journal, 'Find seminars in Hawaii and Arizona, for Debbie!' and drew a heart around it. Three weeks later, the sales manager for a large HVAC Contractor bought my book during the break and asked if I would be willing to come to Honolulu to speak to his team. I replied, "Let me check with my wife; I'll get back to you!" I have since been to Hawaii nine times and Arizona fifteen times. Simple isn't it? I did the same thing with Australia.

Charlie interrupted with a paraphrase. "So I need to be clear on what I want to accomplish, why I want to accomplish it, how badly I want it, and how soon? And I have to write it all down?"

"Yes," his father said, continuing the speaker's story...

Invariably, after every seminar and keynote, during the book signing, someone asks me, 'How did you lose fifty pounds and ten inches off your waist?' I say, 'It started with a simple written goal, clearly defined, written as if it were already so, first person, powerful, personal, and present tense.' Write out a 500 to 1,000-word description of what you want your life and business to look like in five years.

Pausing for effect, Charlie's father said to him, "Son, why not you? You see, goals will add years to your life and life to your years. *Proverbs* says, "Without a vision, the people perish." It really is true. Napoleon Hill said, 'First you work on goals, then they work on you! A goal is dream with a deadline.'"

Gathering his final thoughts, Charlie's dad concluded, "I need to find and thank Coach Wilson. He gave me a great gift by cutting me that November day. My life has never been the same. Son, why not you?"

In a Nutshell

Webster's dictionary defines a GOAL as:

"The object of a person's ambition or effort; an aim or desired result. Objective, end, target, intention, aspiration, dream, desire."

"Nothing can stop the man with the right mental attitude from achieving his goal; nothing on earth can help the man with the wrong mental attitude."

Attributed to Thomas Jefferson

"Obstacles are those frightful things you see when you take your eyes off your goal."

Henry Ford

"Leaders aren't born they are made. And they are made just like anything else, through hard work. And that's the price we'll have to pay to achieve that goal, or any goal."

Vince Lombardi

<u>What</u> is your number-one goal?

How much do you <u>want</u> it?

<u>Why</u> do you want it?

By <u>when</u>?

"Why not you, son?"

CHAPTER FOUR

The Magnificent Seven

By the boys' freshmen year they had evolved into a skilled, mature duo on the court. Charlie and Ben had made the varsity as ninth graders. Their talent belied their age. They did things on the floor the coach had never seen in someone that young. They often took over games. Chip Hilton, their high-school coach, told them at the beginning of the season, *"What you are as a person is far more important than what you are as a basketball player. You guys are leaders. I need you to act like it on and off the floor. Can I count on you?"* The boys replied in unison, *"Yes coach, got it!"*

It was the first winning season the boys basketball team had had in ten years. At mid-season, they were in the middle of the pack at a 7-7 record. Coach Hilton inserted Ben and Charlie into the starting lineup and they proceeded to win seven in a row and make the district playoffs for the first time in school's history. The fans at Jefferson High flocked to the games; there were sold-out crowds every night.

It was heartbreaking when the boys lost the winner to state, *loser goes home* game at the buzzer to the local Catholic powerhouse, O'Dea. Charlie took the loss particularly hard. Coach Hilton put his arm around him and said, "Success is peace of mind which is a direct result of self-satisfaction in knowing you did your best to become the best you are capable of becoming." Charlie forced a smile. "I'm proud of you, Charlie. You and Ben left absolutely nothing on the floor. We'll get them next year!"

Ending the season 14-8 was nothing to be ashamed of given the fact that Jefferson had won only three games the year before.

The next summer the boys worked twice as hard. They shot three hours a day, went to camp for two weeks, and convinced a few of the upperclassmen to do the same. They began to form a special bond on and off the court. You could see it in the way they moved the ball, and encouraged each other from the bench.

Coach Hilton would write quotes on the chalkboard and discuss what they meant to each boy. Charlie's favorites were:

Be true to yourself.

Make each day a masterpiece.

Help others.

Drink deeply from good books.

Make friendship a fine art.

Build a shelter against a rainy day.

The next season the boys advanced to state for the first time in the school's history. The community, the press, even the students jumped on the bandwagon. Winning will do that. Ben took great pride in the fact they had a balanced scoring attack. That season the team had seven leading scorers. It was difficult for teams to focus on just one guy. If you shut down Charlie, Ben would step up. The press dubbed them *The Magnificent Seven*. Charlie was quoted in the paper the day before the semifinal game against their arch rival, O'Dea: *"Today is the only day. Yesterday is gone. Our philosophy is, 'There is no limit to what we can accomplish if we don't care who gets the credit!'"*

Despite playing the best game of the season, the boys fell short and O'Dea went on to win, 57-55. It was a tough loss. Charlie's Dad put his arm around him afterward and said, "Son, the most important thing is family and love. I was proud of you tonight. You gave it your all. You'll get 'em next year!"

Their junior year was something special. They went 18-3 and made it to the championship game. Charlie was 7-8 from the field and hit three straight long range bombs to force the game into overtime. He was in the zone. He was 5-5 from the free-throw line. Coach was shocked when the two seniors on the team went 0-8 from behind the arc and 0-4 from the free throw line. Inexplicably, Charlie never saw the ball after regulation. With the score tied and only fifteen seconds to go, Ben threw the ball into the waiting hands of their star point guard and the clock wound down. Ben added insult to injury when he fouled their star. His opponent calmly sank two free throws and the game was over, 77-75.

It was heartbreaking. Ben took it hard. A local reporter approached him and said, "It seems like you guys are not able to beat this team. How do you feel?"

Ben frowned, paused, and said, "Whatever..."

Charlie put his arm around his best friend. "We have next year." They walked into the locker room holding back the tears.

The only thing Coach Hilton said in the locker room was, "Success is never final; failure is never fatal. It's courage that counts. Boys, more proud of you I could not be. I wouldn't trade this team for ten O'Dea's. Hold your heads high. We will win it all next year!"

There is a strong belief among great coaches that there is a process to winning and building a championship team, that it requires a change not only in belief but in effort and results. It has four stages:

First, you lose big.

Second, you lose close.

Third, you win close.

Fourth, you win big.

Next year, Jefferson would win big. It was as simple as that.

Charlie and Ben came up with a simple plan in the off-season. "We will play together EVERY DAY, working on our passing, rebounding, execution, free throws, everything. Next year, we go 25-0!" They examined the schedule. Printing it out, they wrote a big "W" next to each game. They hung a picture of the State Championship Trophy on the locker room wall, "Jefferson High School State Champs, 25-0" in big block letters across the top, and they listed ten reasons why they wanted it. As the team entered and left the locker room each practice, every player touched the poster, slapping it hard with their palms, yelling, "State champs!"

Every week a new quote appeared on the chalkboard:

Knocked down seven times, stand up eight!
It's not how far you fall, but how high you bounce that counts!
It's not what happens, it's how we respond!

Jefferson roared through the season, making it all the way to the championship game, against—who else?—O'Dea. The game was televised. The whole state was watching. The standing-room-only crowd was riveted by Charlie and Ben who dazzled them with pinpoint passing, flawless execution, and supreme effort. As the clock wound down, with the crowd counting down the seconds aloud, Ben looked up at the scoreboard and smiled. Redemption. 83-60 Jefferson... state champs! Ben fell to his knees as his teammates dog-piled on top of him. He was voted MVP. He had made all of his free throws, 15-15; he scored twenty-one points; had eleven assists; and ten steals. A triple double! With the net around his neck, Charlie by his side, with his long arm draped around his best friend, they relished their victory. The photograph on the front page of the Seattle Times's sports section captured that magical moment. Words could not express how Ben felt. His smile said it all. He did NOT say "Whatever..."

Behind the boys stood two cheerleaders, twins: Katie and Kim. Neither boy knew it then, but they would play big parts in the next chapter of their lives.

A week later, the top junior college coach in the state offered Ben and Charlie a full scholarship. They were taking their skills to the next level.

In a Nutshell

"Success is peace of mind which is a direct result of self-satisfaction in knowing you did your best to become the best you are capable of becoming."

"Today is the only day. Yesterday is gone."

"Success is never final, failure is never fatal. It's courage that counts."

"The most important things in the world are family and love."

"Be true to yourself. Make each day a masterpiece. Help others. Drink deeply from good books. Make friendship a fine art. Build a shelter against a rainy day."

"What you are as a person is far more important than what you are as a basketball player."

"First, you lose big.

Second, you lose close.

Third, you win close.

FREEDOM FROM FAT

Fourth, you win big."

"Knocked down seven times, stand up eight!"

"It's not how far you fall, but how high you bounce that counts!"

CHAPTER FIVE

Higher Learning

Shoreline Community College had just hired a new young coach. He was single, had played on a state-championship high-school team, a Division 3 national-championship college team as a point guard, and now had his dream job. Head coach. And boy could he sell. Kevin Thomas could charm a cat off a fish truck. In his first summer of recruiting, he had signed his all-state backcourt of Charlie at the two (shooting guard) and Ben at the one (point guard) and two other freshman, who played the three and four respectively, had been all-conference and were solid defenders. He snagged Big Joe Turner, a six-foot-nine, 253-pound, twenty-three-year-old center that had been in the Air Force for four years. They reeled off fifteen wins in a row to start the season. Could this team get up and down the floor! These boys all came from winning programs; they gave 100% every game, every play. They were fun to watch.

Kim and Katie Babbington, the twins, followed the boys to Shoreline. Only their family could tell them apart. They dressed alike until their senior year of high school, mostly to confuse people. Kim swooned over Ben, and Katie had already told her sister, "Hands off my sweet Charlie; he's mine. One day I'm going to marry that man!" She would say that to anyone who would listen.

In high school, Ben and Charlie never had time for girls. Ben excelled in the sciences, math, and shop, earning a respectable 3.6 GPA.

He did, however, struggle with English and debate. Charlie, on the other hand, had all A's except for math (he got a B), for an impressive 3.8 GPA. As on the court, so it was off: they complemented each other with respective strengths. Basketball and homework. No time for girls. Oh, how things change…

Their dating started innocently enough, bumping into one another in the cafeteria, seeing each other in the halls. One day, the twins approached the boys at lunch and tossed an envelope onto the table. "We want you to take us to this. You can buy us Big Macs and fries before the show. We'll pick you up at 5:30 tonight," and they walked away. Their phone number was on the outside of the envelope. Inside were four tickets to *Rocky*.

These girls were not used to hearing no from anyone. They were tall, five-foot-ten, with long blond hair, curled slightly, dropping just below their shoulders. Their piercing blue eyes were mesmerizing, and oh, yes, they were fit. In addition to cheerleading, they played volleyball, ran track and were in drama club in high school. Katie had been homecoming Queen and Kim was runner up.

"Kinda pushy don't you think?" Charlie said.

"Whatever…" replied Ben. This *whatever* was different. It held no sarcasm or negativity. It was almost a whisper.

Charlie laughed. "You're a trip, bro! You so dig Kimmy. She has the hots for you."

"Me?" Ben replied with mock incredulity. "I've seen the way you look at Katie. At least, I think it's Katie. To be honest, half the time I can't tell 'em apart. Kimmy wears a lot of scarfs. That's the only way I really know."

"You wanna go out with them?" Charlie asked.

"Whatever… You?"

"Why not?" Charlie said. "Could be fun."

That was it. From the first date on, Kim and Katie were always by the boys' sides. After games, at the mall, on weekends. It got serious fast. They say the first cut is the deepest. This one required stitches.

That season ended on a high note, final four, losing the championship game at the buzzer. The good news was they had all five starters back, plus two more star players from Jefferson High, a six-foot-ten backup center and lightening quick point guard who could shoot and pass. Their sophomore year, the Shoreline Samuari went 32-0 on the way to the school's first NWAC Championship. The trophy was as big a VW Bug! If you look closely you can see the twins in the corner of the picture with their arms in the air.

Charlie accepted a D-2 scholarship to Western Washington University in bucolic little Bellingham, Washington, a winning program with a proud and rich tradition. He declared his major to be business with minors in English and journalism. Charlie loved school and earned a 4.0 his final two years. He devoured the assigned books and wrote in his journal constantly. When he wasn't playing ball or hanging out with Katie, who followed him to Bellingham, he was diligently writing or reading. He began capturing his own favorite quotes in his journal, something every coach he admired had done:

"The books you don't read won't help."

Jim Rohn

"The man who does not read has no advantage over the man who cannot read."

Mark Twain (attributed)

"If we encounter a man of rare intellect, we should ask him what books he reads."

Ralph Waldo Emerson

FREEDOM FROM FAT

"It's what you read when you don't have to that determines what you will be when you can't help it."

Oscar Wilde

"Make it a rule to never give a child a book you would not read yourself."

George Bernard Shaw

Ben, on the other hand, accepted a job with Kimmy's Dad's company and began an apprenticeship to become an HVAC technician. School was always a means to an end for him. Working with his hands appealed to his nature. Besides, he had big plans. Ben's dad, Steve, originally objected to his decision saying, "Guys who sit down when they work make more money than guys who stand up." Steve knew from experience. He had been a telephone installer for thirty years. Nonetheless, Ben's mind was made up. Besides, he would see Kimmy every day. Her father promised an upwardly mobile path for Ben. He was the son he never had.

The future looked bright for both boys. The best was yet to come.

In a Nutshell

"The books you don't read won't help."

Jim Rohn

"The man who does not read has no advantage over the man who cannot read."

Mark Twain (attributed)

"If we encounter a man of rare intellect, we should ask him what books he reads."

Ralph Waldo Emerson

"It's what you read when you don't have to that determines what you will be when you can't help it."

Oscar Wilde

"Make it a rule to never give a child a book you would not read yourself."

George Bernard Shaw

CHAPTER SIX

The Salad Days

Ben and Charlie had no idea their paths were about to cross again. The next two years were the salad days for both of them. Despite their youth, their futures were so bright it burned the eyes of the people around them. There was no limit on how good they could get, depending upon how hard they were willing to work "off the court". And man, did they work.

Ben loved the service business. It appealed to his analytical nature. He flew through his apprenticeship, graduating with "Apprentice of the Year" honors. Kim's father had high expectations. He was tougher on him than he was on his other employees. "Ben, you know why I'm so hard on you, right?"

Ben wanted to say, "Whatever..." but resisted the temptation. "Of course. It's not a problem. Playing for Chip Hilton and Kevin Thomas prepared me for hard work and long hours. I love this job. I'll do whatever you need me to."

Ben taped an index card on the dashboard of his service truck. It said **"F.I.L.O."** which stood for **"First In, Last Out."** It was his motto for hard work. He arrived at the shop every morning at 06:00 to clean and organize his truck. He reviewed his paperwork to make certain it was complete. He even created an acronym for *that:* **"N.O.D.S."** It stood for **"Neat, On-Time, Detailed, and Signed."** Ben was fastidious that way, an I-dotting T-crosser. Point guards are coaches on the floor. They lead by able example. Ben was simply being a point guard at work. Despite his age, the other guys respected him. He loved his job. He was a model employee. Everyone knew he was destined for ownership and not because he was dating the boss's daughter. There is a saying in business: "No one gets promoted. You get bigger than your job and eventually get lifted up." Ben was quickly becoming bigger than his job.

Meanwhile, up in Bellingham, Charlie had finished up his senior year for the Vikings as MVP of the league and earned All-American honors. He had offers to play overseas. At a job fair one day, a representative from Western Electric, his father's company, offered him a job as a sales representative. It was too good to pass up. Hearing Ben's father's words echoing in his brain, "Guys who sit down when they work make more money than guys who stand up," he decided to forgo his plans to play overseas and accept the job. He was sold on the idea with a single sentence: "The very things that made you a great basketball player will also make you a great salesperson." Upon graduation, he went to work for Western Electric.

He was sent to an intense three-day sales school in Pittsburgh. The presenter, Dan O'Hara, was a former super-salesman with an engaging, humorous, and interactive teaching style. He reminded Charlie of his college coach; he wanted to be just like him. He took fifty pages of notes and, on the third day, he made a presentation that received a rousing ovation from his peers. His future was bright indeed. On the final night, Dan O'Hara put his arm around Charlie at dinner and said, "One day, YOU will be teaching this seminar! If you ever need a job, call me. Stay in touch." Charlie made some notes in his journal on the flight home:

"Sales is a numbers game. If my boss asks me to make two proposals a week, do five!"

"Get great at qualifying the prospect. Ask open-ended Questions (Who, What, Where, When, How, and Why) and actively listen. Dominate the listening in every conversation."

"To create a killer proposal, include pictures, cost justifications, attributable quotes from delighted clients, detailed descriptions of the work we will perform, and end it with a "Choice of Yeses." Change the buying dynamic from IF they will buy to WHICH option will they choose."

Ben listened to audio cassettes while he drove around. He called this on-the-road learning *Windshield University*. He was a street scholar! He faithfully listened to Zig Ziglar, Earl Nightingale, Wayne Dyer, and Denis Waitley. Their ideas fired his imagination. He even began to keep a journal of things he learned on the job: wiring diagrams, piping concepts, Ohm's Law, the latent heat of evaporation, and painful lessons learned the hard way, like the time he was nearly electrocuted in the walk-in freezer. The title of this entry simply said, "NEVER want to do this again..." and then it described what happened and what he should have done differently. Ben set goals and kept them to himself. By the end of his second year as a tech, he was the top producer of project and service agreements. He was selling more than the guy who had been hired to sell, all the while generating sixty hours of billable time per week as a tech. Bob Babbington could not have been more proud.

In the meantime, an hour up Interstate 5, Charlie took to sales like a duck to water. He made 150% of sales plan his first year, 200% his second, 300% his third, and earned more money in a month than his father had earned in a year. He was getting phone calls every week from recruiters. The sales manager of Bellevue's largest Mercedes dealer even offered him a job in the middle of Charlie's sales presentation. His confidence grew every week. His final year at Western Electric, he enjoyed a 75% close ratio. His favorite quote at the end of a presentation was, "If you like the previews, you'll love the movie!"

One Friday, the receptionist handed him a pink While You Were Out note. It simply said, "Please call Bob ASAP." It was from Kimmy's father. "Can we have lunch Charlie?" Bob asked over the phone.

"You bet," is all Charlie said.

FREEDOM FROM **FAT**

At lunch, Bob offered Charlie a job in sales. It was a very tempting offer, a nice salary with the chance to earn much more in commissions. Moreover, a chance to play on the same team as Ben again. It didn't talk him long to decide.

Another championship was on the way...

In a Nutshell

"F.I.L.O." which stood for "First In, Last Out." It was his motto for hard work.

"No one gets promoted. You get bigger than your job and eventually get lifted up."

"Sale is a numbers game. If my boss asks me to make two proposals a week, do five!"

"Get great at qualifying the prospect. Ask open-ended questions (Who, What, Where, When, How, and Why) and actively listen. Dominate the listening in every conversation."

"Join Windshield University (to become a street scholar)."

"If you like the previews, you'll love the movie!"

"Another championship was on the way..."

CHAPTER SEVEN

Turning the Corner

By this time, the business had become a family affair. Ben was promoted to service manager. He supervised twenty technicians, an overworked dispatcher (Kim's Aunt June), two field foremen (Charlie's cousins), a parts manager (Ben's little brother Brian), and two guys in the warehouse. He was indeed doing all he could and then some. He and Kim (she asked Ben to stop calling her Kimmy or she would call him "Benji;" It stopped that day!) had been married for two years now and they were expecting their first child. Kim managed accounts receivable; Katie, her sister, took on accounts payable. Kim's mother, Edna, managed the office.

Reading and practicing simple human-relations principles on a daily basis kept Ben's wife happy and the employees delighted. Morale was at an all-time high, turnover at an all-time low. When one of Ben's guys would come into his office with a gripe, he would listen actively, nod, occasionally say "Uh-huh," or "And what did he say..." and then listen some more. Upon completion, he would use the Socratic method and ask, "So what are you gonna do?" More often than not, his guys would figure it out on their own. He was simply being a sounding board. They loved him for it.

Once, his top tech, Daniel Johnson, came into the office with a letter. "Ben, I screwed up, I made a mistake on a large project; it's gonna cost the company over $100,000! I am so sorry, I know I let you down."

He handed Ben a letter of resignation. Ben, with the most solemn expression he could muster, read the letter with mock interest.

When he was done, he looked right at Dan, smiled, and tore up the letter. "Are you nuts? I just invested one-hundred grand training you. Now go make me some money! And Dan, do me a favor, Make NEW mistakes, will ya?!" Dan flopped back in his chair with a giant sigh of relief. Ben added, "You have anything to say?"

Dan jumped up, smiled and said, "Whatever..." and left. That was Ben "Franklin" living up to his namesake.

Charlie was rocking and rolling on the other side of the office. Sales had increased 35% a year for three straight years and in the first quarter alone, he had already made his sales plan. He was projecting a 50% increase by the end of the fiscal year. His only concern? Could Ben find the right kind of guys (he called them O.K.G.'s, *Our Kinda Guys*) fast enough to keep up with sales. It was a genuine concern. He had plans to hire another sales person this year so he could invest more time in strategic planning, succession planning, and vacation planning. His wife, Katie, was also pregnant, expecting within weeks of Kim. Those twins, they had to do everything together.

Charlie was in charge of training. Every week he would choose a principle, find a quote, and tell a story. This particular week the word he wrote on the flip chart was "WORK!" followed by the quote, "You know it's funny, the harder and smarter I work, the luckier I get and the more money I make." He followed with a story...

Many years ago, a preacher rode down a narrow country lane, his horse strolling at an easy walk. As he rounded a turn, the elms and oaks parted to reveal the most beautiful farmstead he had ever seen. The house and barn were freshly painted, the lawn trim and manicured, the beds overflowing with gorgeous marigolds. In the pasture, Holstein cattle grazed while two dogs romped by the farmyard gate. The whole scene was the ideal of rural life, like a print from Currier and Ives.

As he marveled at the view, the farmer stepped out of his home and approached the preacher. "Hello to you," said the farmer. "What brings you all the way out here?"

"Why, I was just passing through on my way to a new church in the next town when I was struck by the beauty of your farm. Sir, yours is the most perfect farm I have seen. I'm sure you are grateful to the good Lord for all he has given you."

"Indeed, we are," said the farmer, wiping the sweat from his brow. "But you should have seen it when the Lord had it all to himself!"

Though his employees laughed at the punchline, they understood Charlie's point. They knew every story Charlie told had a point or principle. Charlie continued:

"Each of us is given a plot of earth, some ground we can call our own. What are going to do with yours? It's not what we have, it's what we do with it. The greatest law in the universe is the Law of Sowing and Reaping. Cause and effect. Now what do we need to improve at our company? Write down your ideas on the index cards in front of you. We will put all the ideas on this flip chart and vote on the best one to apply. The person who comes up with the number-one Idea gets dinner and a movie on the company OR a $75 gift card!

That's how Charlie got his employees involved in growing the company, taking responsibility for new ideas and going the extra-mile. He rewarded the behavior he wanted repeated. He would hand out $20 bills for guys who went the extra mile on jobs, or if a customer wrote a letter of praise it went on the "Wall of Fame." The employees acted like it was THEIR company. They had psychological ownership. Ben and Charlie understood the deepest craving in the human condition is the need to be appreciated.

One day, over lunch, Bob said to Ben and Charlie, "What you two have done in three years defies comprehension. I'm holding you guys back. The best thing I can do is get out of your way. I propose you guys buy me out, I will retain 51% for five years, at that point you will buy me out completely. Each of you gets 24.5% now and you become 50-50 partners in five short years. It goes without saying, my daughters own half of all you have. I know I don't need to say that but my attorney insisted."

Ben was blown away. Charlie smiled. He had set a goal in five years to own a service company. He reached in his briefcase and handed Bob his goal list. He was two years ahead of plan. Bob frowned, then laughed aloud. "You two are way ahead of me, as usual. I know this is the right thing to do. I want to take Edna around the world. I want to spoil those grandkids, buy an Airstream, and take them to Disneyland, Yosemite, the Grand Canyon, Mt. Rushmore and much much more. I want you guys to talk it over with the twins. Think about it, and let's talk again in a couple of weeks."

Charlie grabbed the bill, "I got lunch!"

Ben said, "Whatever..."

In a Nutshell

"I must ask myself a dozen times a day: What am I modeling?"

"But you should have seen this place when he had it all to himself."

"Now what do we need to improve here at our company?"

"That's how Charlie got his employees involved in growing the company, taking responsibility for new ideas and going the extra-mile. He rewarded the behavior he wanted repeated."

"Create a 'Wall of Fame' in your office with pictures of people and praise for performance."

"The deepest craving in the human condition is the need to be appreciated."

CHAPTER EIGHT

Walk Your Talk

"Too many people and organizations do not walk their talk," Ben said to Charlie one day. "The words on the wall don't match the behavior in the hall. Few people actually put their money where their mouth is. Rarely do they live their values." Ben had just finished reading The *Autobiography of Benjamin Franklin*.

Surprised he had read a book (as opposed to listening to it on cassette) Charlie inquired, "So how do we get to the application level and live our values?" Ben proceeded to give him a history lesson.

"Ben Franklin was a pioneer," he said with passion. "He was the first man to systemize behavioral change. In his late twenties, he sought something he called *Moral Perfection*. On July 1, 1733, he listed his Thirteen Virtues, described and laid out in a journal on a kind of early spreadsheet. For Ben, this quest was a simple system for living his values; a way to make precepts, principles, positive qualities live and breath in his life. First he listed them in his journal.

1. **Temperance**

2. **Silence**

3. **Order**

4. **Resolution**

5. Frugality

6. Industry

7. Sincerity

8. Justice

9. Moderation

10. Cleanliness

11. Tranquility

12. Chastity

13. Humility

In his own words, he describes his quest and system:

"My intention being to acquire the habitude of all these virtues, I judg'd it would be well not to distract my attention by attempting the whole at once, but to fix it on one of them at a time; and, when I should be master of that, then to proceed to another, and so on, till I should have gone thro' the thirteen...

"I made a little book, in which I allotted a page for each of the virtues. I rul'd each page with red ink, so as to have seven columns, one for each day of the week, marking each column with a letter for the day. I cross'd these columns with thirteen red lines, marking the beginning of each line with the first letter of one of the virtues, on which line, and in its proper column, I might mark, by a little black spot, every fault I found upon examination to have been committed respecting that virtue upon that day. I determined to give a week's strict attention to each of the virtues successively. Thus, in the first week, my great guard was to avoid every the least offense against Temperance, leaving the other virtues to their ordinary chance, only marking every evening the faults of the day.

"I could go thro' a course compleat in thirteen weeks, and four courses in a year. And like him who, having a garden to weed,

does not attempt to eradicate all the bad herbs at once, which would exceed his reach and his strength, but works on one of the beds at a time..."

So it went for Ben Franklin over the next fifty years. Mastery over defects of character and the systematic adoption of positive qualities and virtues."

"Now it's our turn?" Charlie asked.

"Yes!" Ben replied. "Let's brainstorm our list." A couple of hours later they were done. They created their Thirteen Virtues, listed and described in order of their proper sequence. "We will strive for Moral Perfection, moreover, we will also seek Balance, Wealth and Peace of Mind in the application of these virtues!"

"Spoken like a true coach," Charlie said.

1. **Study**

2. **Humility**

3. **Industry**

4. **Order**

5. **Frugality**

6. **Resolution**

7. **Silence**

8. **Sincerity**

9. **Wellness**

10. **Forgiveness**

11. **Humor**

12. **Sartorial Splendor**

13. **Temperance**

Just like his namesake, Ben wrote out a rough draft, a paragraph describing the change in behavior. It was magical. They knew they had created something challenging yet unique.

1. **Study**

   Begin my day with "The Hour of Power." <u>Read</u> for twenty minutes in a book or magazine in alignment with my number-one goal at that time. Authors who have done what I want to do and been where I want to go... <u>Think</u> for twenty minutes on that very goal. Write it at the top of the page in my journal in the form of a question and list as many ideas as I can think of that day... <u>Plan</u> for twenty minutes, "What are the six most important things I need to do today?" Estimate, "How long will each task will take?" Then list them in order of importance.

2. **Humility**

   Study great leaders. Abraham Lincoln, Lawrence of Arabia, Gandhi, Martin Luther King, Nelson Mandela, Robert E. Lee. When it comes time to receive the credit, give it away. When it's time to accept the blame, assume it all. This simple discipline will improve every relationship I have in my life. Be the change I would like to see in others.

3. **Industry**

   Work on first things first, one thing at a time and finish what I start. Work doing what I love, ten hours a day, from 5:00 am to 3:00 pm, Sundays off. Sundays are for study, spiritual text, reading *The New York Times*, a biography of someone I admire, personal and professional reflection in my journal.

4. **Order**

   A place for everything, and everything in its place. Balance is the watchword. Let all things have their time and place each day; let each part of your business have its time: marketing, sales, finance, relationships, skill development, etc.

5. **Frugality**

Tithe 10% of all I earn and never touch it. Ask myself before I spend money, "Do I really need this?" Learn to delay gratification. Set goals to find the things that I need for free (or at least heavily discounted).

6. **Resolution**

Resolve to perform what you ought; perform without fail what you resolve. Keep my word to myself each day. "To thine own self be true!" Do what I say. Congruence.

7. **Silence**

Be other-centered. Actively listen in every conversation. Remember W.A.I.T. (Why Am I Talking?) Summarize only after the other person is done. Think twice, speak once or not at all. There is great power in silence. I never learn anything of real value when I am speaking, only when I listen. Be content to understand first, then to be understood.

8. **Sincerity**

Be authentic, genuine, real. Demonstrate true empathy. When I do speak, make it from the heart, from my own experience. First-person warnings or third-person examples. Tell stories that matter, that teach, that mean something.

9. **Wellness**

Exercise every day. Walk, swim, yoga, weights, basketball, meditation. Eat clean and small, healthy portions of *SuperFoods*. Meat, vegetables, and fruit. Avoid processed foods, sugar, excessive carbohydrates. Drink lots of water. "No food tastes as good as skinny feels."

10. **Forgiveness**

Life is too short to *be-little*. Resentment is like drinking poison and expecting the other person to die. Forgive and forget. Move on. If the resentment persists, pray for that person for two weeks.

11. **Humor**

Laugh every day. Don't take myself too seriously. Laughing releases endorphins, improves circulation and memory, and makes for pleasant conversations. Study humor and improv: Self-effacing is best, make fun of myself. Observe, acknowledge, heighten, then call back to the beginning and summarize.

12. **Sartorial Splendor**

Clothes really do make the man. Plan each day's wardrobe. Dress just a little nicer than the meeting demands. Mix and match. Begin with the hat. I can always loosen my tie or remove my sport coat. We get one chance to make a positive first impression.

13. **Temperance**

All things in moderation. Have a positive expectation of my future. Be grateful for my blessings. Give thanks in written form (postcards, sticky notes, etc.) Eat not to dullness. Avoid alcohol and drugs.

Energized and in the zone, Charlie said, "I resolve to put these on index cards and focus on one virtue a week for thirteen weeks. Carry the card with me. Look at it several times a day. Reflect each night upon the application of that virtue. Give myself a reward for a day well spent." Now it was Charlie's turn to be the coach. Pausing to collect his thoughts, he continued, "Furthermore, I am going to write each of these virtues in the form of a third-person goal. *"Charles Dickens Smith does all things in moderation. He has a positive expectation of his future.*

He is grateful for all of his blessings. He give thanks each day by writing five postcards a day to people in his life."

"Charlie," Ben said, "this is powerful stuff. You know I am going to hold you accountable to live these values and goals." Charlie just smiled.

After writing all of this down, Charles and Ben felt a giant weight lift off of them. They knew in their hearts they were on the right path. Charlie captured a few quotes in his journal and showed them to Ben:

"The aim of education is the knowledge, not of facts, but of values."

William S. Burroughs, Author

"Achievement of your happiness is the only moral purpose of your life, and that happiness, not pain or mindless self-indulgence, is the proof of your moral integrity, since it is the proof and the result of your loyalty to the achievement of your values."

Ayn Rand, Author, Philosopher

"When your values are clear to you, making decisions becomes easier."

Roy Disney, Walt's Brother and Business Partner

"A people that values its privileges above its principles soon loses both."

Dwight D. Eisenhower, US President

"Now it was time to do the same for the company... The Dynamic Duo created posters titled *Company Vision, Values, Goals* and mounted them on the walls. They created mini versions on laminated cards and gave one to each employee. They were determined to set the example by living up to their thirteen virtues. And they did.

In a Nutshell

1. Study

2. Humility

3. Industry

4. Order

5. Frugality

6. Resolution

7. Silence

8. Sincerity

9. Wellness

10. Forgiveness

11. Humor

12. Sartorial Splendor

13. Temperance

"Achievement of your happiness is the only moral purpose of your life, and that happiness, not pain or mindless self-indulgence, is the proof of your moral integrity, since it is the proof and the result of your loyalty to the achievement of your values."

Ayn Rand, Author, Philosopher

"When your values are clear to you, making decisions becomes easier."

Roy Disney, Walt's Brother and Business Partner

"A people that values its privileges above its principles soon loses both."

Dwight D. Eisenhower, US President

-Part Two-
Forward

CHAPTER NINE

The Wake-Up Call

Ben had a way with words. He was a regular guy who used regular language. He was authentic. His hero was a catcher, Yankee great Yogi Berra. He even had a picture of him in his office, smiling with that big gap in his teeth. They were built the same, 5'-9", 195 pounds of muscle. He quoted him all the time.

If you don't know where you are going... you might not get there.

Baseball is ninety percent mental. The other half is physical.

You can observe a lot just by watching.

Little League baseball is a very good thing because it keeps the parents off the streets.

I never said most of the things I said.

When you come to a fork in the road, take it.

I ain't in no slump... I just ain't hitting!

These quotes rolled off of Ben's tongue at the most opportune times, often when he was talking to his techs. He was great at one-on-one, yet despised speaking to an audience bigger than four or five people.

Ben was a hugger. He loved people. Prior to hugging one of his techs he would say, "Come on, press the laundry!" While he was hugging, he'd say, "This will ruin every hug you'll ever have for the rest of your life; when you hug someone, the trick is to see who lets go first." The crazy thing is, he never intended to be funny, he just was.

Ben wasn't really a drinker. He'd nurse a single beer with some guys and then go home. Charlie on the other hand, loved booze a little too much. "Good Time Charlie" was his nickname, especially after three or four drinks. Some say it was his competitive nature. Others said it was in his genes. His father had a little problem with alcohol and it almost cost him his marriage. He stopped in time. His dad used to say, "I gotta hit a meeting." We never really knew what that meant, but he was different after that. People really loved Charlie's dad, Chuck, Sr.

Kim and Ben had just had their second child. Their oldest, Chuck, was a precocious little four-year-old. Their newborn daughter was the apple of Ben's eye. Ben was proud of the house he had built for his growing family. Despite all of his responsibilities as VP of Operations, he found the time to be the general contractor on the house of his dreams. 6,000 square feet, four bedrooms, a swimming pool, and a hot tub. One day, while he was shoveling birch bark from the back of his truck, he felt a shooting pain in his chest. He dropped the shovel, lost his balance, and tumbled to the ground. His head hit a rock and he was out cold. Kim found him unconscious and immediately called 911. She cried as she held him, rocking him back and forth until the ambulance came.

Ben was in a coma and Kim was there with him day and night. Charlie never left his side, catching a few winks in the chair across from his sister-in-law. Kim cried until no more tears would come. Charlie talked to him, reminding him of all the things they had accomplished, story after story. He refused to give up.

The doctors informed the family that a heart attack had forced Ben to lose his balance. He had gained five pounds a year over the last ten years since he quit playing basketball. It happens to middle-aged athletes. And Ben liked to eat. No one ever said he was fat, but people described him as *sturdy, stout,* and *a big guy.* The reality was that he was obese. He had a gut. He ate whatever he wanted and the beer didn't help. His doctor had warned him to lose thirty pounds. He would shake his head and say, "Whatever..."

A week later, Ben woke up, smiled, saw his family standing around him with forced smiles, and said, "I love you guys. I had such big plans..." And then he was gone.

Rites of passage are defined as ceremonies or events marking life's important stages, especially birth, puberty, marriage, and death. Charlie had been there for every one of Ben's except one. The state championship and Ben's MVP trophy, his first kiss, falling in love with Kimmy, the prom, marriage, the early business success, and now his passing.

Shakespeare wrote, "Cowards die many times before their deaths; the valiant never taste of death but once." Ben was valiant. Ben worked so hard, with so much passion, he crammed two lifetimes into a third of one.

"No one should die this early," Charlie thought to himself. He saw how hard Ben's dad took it. "No one should outlive his children," he said.

Marcus Aurelius said, "It's not death that a man should fear, but he should fear never beginning to live." Ben lived.

Men of age object too much, consult too long, adventure too little, repent too soon, and seldom drive business home to the full period, but content themselves with a mediocrity of success. Life's tragedy is that we get old too soon and wise too late. Not so for Ben. He was wise so soon, an old soul in a young body.

Ben was born three weeks premature. He was always in a hurry, as it turns out, for everything.

Charlie thought to himself, "What are we going to do? How will we get over this?" Grief is time out of mind, a kind of suspended animation.

And then he heard a voice say, "We carry on." Kim put her arm around her brother-in-law. "We're family." She enrolled the family, and anyone else who wanted to go, in a grief-counseling program. Talking about pain and loss cuts it in half. And talk they did...

In a Nutshell

If you don't know where you are going... you might not get there.

Baseball is ninety percent mental. The other half is physical.

You can observe a lot just by watching.

Come on, press the laundry!

Cowards die many times before their deaths; the valiant never taste of death but once.

It's not death that a man should fear, but he should fear never beginning to live.

Whatever; Whenever, Wherever... We carry on!

CHAPTER TEN

Grief and Closure

Ben's memorial was an event, a huge gathering that surprised many people for both its attendance and duration. 500 people showed up and it lasted over three hours. When guests were invited to say a few words, dozens of people came to the lectern to share their memories of Ben.

Kim read a poem:

> *Do not stand at my grave and weep*
>
> *I am not there; I do not sleep.*
>
> *I am a thousand winds that blow,*
>
> *I am the diamond glints on snow,*
>
> *I am the sun on ripened grain,*
>
> *I am the gentle autumn rain.*
>
> *When you awaken in the morning's hush*
>
> *I am the swift uplifting rush*
>
> *Of quiet birds in circled flight.*
>
> *I am the soft stars that shine at night.*
>
> *Do not stand at my grave and cry,*
>
> *I am not there; I did not die.*

Katie sang the Cole Porter classic "Ev'ry Time We Say Goodbye."

Every time we say goodbye, I die a little,

Every time we say goodbye, I wonder why a little,

Why the Gods above me, who must be in the know.

Think so little of me, they allow you to go.

Charlie was the last person to speak. He had prepared his speech for days, putting down on paper exactly what he wanted to say. He cleared his throat and began:

"Someone once said that we die twice, the first time when we pass and the second time when people stop talking about us. Being forgotten is a kind of second death. I will never forget my friend and business partner, Benjamin Franklin Jones. He was the finest man I ever knew. He was my best friend for over thirty years. We all must be careful how we remember people, especially old friends. A man's life cannot be summed up in a ten-minute tribute. Those things are the bricks. It's not the bricks, it's the mortar, the stuff you can't see, that makes up a man's life. It seems some of us don't get to dictate our destiny."

Charlie paused to compose himself, and continued,

"This has been the hardest thing I have ever gone through. Like many of you, I've been through all five stages of grief: denial, anger, bargaining, depression, acceptance. As we navigate through these extreme emotions, we jump around, in no particular order, like a pinball in a machine. Emotions are all over the place as we cry, laugh, or get mad. Then we turn to what we know for solace and comfort. For me and Ben, it has always been family. When someone you love dies, you don't lose them all at once. You lose them in little pieces, like how the mail eventually stops coming for you after you are gone. What I tried to remember was why I liked him so much, what it was that drew people to him. Here is my short list:

10 Great Things about Ben Jones:

1) He was and is the glue that binds together all the diverse personalities in our crazy family and business. The voice of reason and objectivity. He did that on every team he played with. He was our captain.

2) He was a positive force of nature. He loved people, but on his terms, one-on-one. He didn't like public attention or crowds. He would think this funeral was all too much. When you first met him you would think him shy. He wasn't, just cautious. Once you were on his team, he always had an encouraging word, a thoughtful gesture, or a big hug.

3) He loved his family. They adored him.

4) He was curious, always learning and growing. Never satisfied with the status quo. Always wanting to get better.

5) He was persistent. A bulldog. Fearless, brave, courageous.

6) He was the most competitive guy I ever knew, basketball, business, shoot, even cribbage or Monopoly. He hated to lose.

7) His laugh. Once, in third grade, I made milk come out his nose. He was a quick laugher.

8) His Attitude. The whole "Whatever" thing was an act. What he really meant is "I will do WHATEVER it takes for us to succeed!"

9) His commitment to the team. He was so unselfish. He often had a good shot, but passed it to me for a better one. He led us to many a championship.

10) Finally, he never wanted the credit, ever. He always gave it away. If we lost, at anything, he assumed the blame. I guess it was his humility and love that stands out to me the most. Yes... the love.

FREEDOM FROM FAT

Robert Browning Hamilton wrote,

I walked a mile with Pleasure;

She chatted all the way;

But left me none the wiser

For all she had to say.

I walked a mile with Sorrow;

And ne'er a word said she;

But, oh! The things I learned from her,

When Sorrow walked with me.

"Up until today, I always took for granted two phrases we use every day: 'See you later' and 'Goodbye.' For as long as I can remember, Ben used to say, 'See you later, Chuck.' Now I know, 'Goodbye' means 'I won't see you later for the rest of my life.' We are gathered here today to say 'Goodbye.'"

Mark Twain once wrote, "Let us endeavor so to live that when we come to die even the undertaker will be sorry." Ben did just that.

A hush fell over the gathering, as if he was holding his breath for everyone, waiting to exhale. After a long pause, he continued. "I know what Ben would say if he were here. Everyone say it with me..." In unison, 500 people shouted, "WHATEVER!"

As the crowd left the church, Charlie was walking with his family when a goldfinch appeared, swirling around them, eventually landing on a branch. It sang the sweetest song anyone had ever heard. We stood in silence. And then it was gone. Kim said, "That was Benji the Bird. Came back to say thank you and goodbye."

In a Nutshell

Every time we say goodbye.

A man's life cannot be summed up in a ten-minute tribute. Those things are the bricks. It's not the bricks, it's the mortar, the stuff you can't see, that makes up a man's life.

> *Do not stand at my grave and weep*
> *I am not there; I do not sleep.*
> *I am a thousand winds that blow,*
> *I am the diamond glints on snow,*
> *I am the sun on ripened grain,*
> *I am the gentle autumn rain.*
> *When you awaken in the morning's hush*
> *I am the swift uplifting rush*
> *Of quiet birds in circled flight.*
> *I am the soft stars that shine at night.*
> *Do not stand at my grave and cry,*
> *I am not there; I did not die.*

FREEDOM FROM FAT

I walked a mile with Pleasure;

She chatted all the way;

But left me none the wiser

For all she had to say.

I walked a mile with Sorrow;

And ne'er a word said she;

But, oh! The things I learned from her,

When Sorrow walked with me.

CHAPTER ELEVEN

Benjamin Franklin Jones University

Ben believed passionately about training and education. Perhaps because he stopped after two years of college to begin his apprenticeship, a part of him felt unfinished. Regardless, Charlie knew he must carry on with Ben's tradition of education, both personal and professional. He asked himself,

"What did the university I attended leave out of the curriculum that is most vital for success in this business and more importantly, the people I serve at the company?"

He only had to look at Ben's passions and behavior to find the answers:

1) Change

2) Teamwork

3) Customer Service

He would add Wellness to the list later... but I digress.

These three topics, Change, Teamwork, and Customer Service would serve as a foundation for what HE would teach. A triangle. An operating philosophy. A foundation.

C.H.A.N.G.E. Charlie determined, would be an acronym. It stood for:

C = Courageous Calm

H = Honorable Habits

A = Attitude & Altitude

N = New Next

G = Giant Goals

E = Eager Edict

Charlie created his outline and formula for creating curriculum by taking a complex subject and simplifying it so everyone could understand it. From there he used process to get everyone engaged and involved. Topic, definition, quotes, story, exercise. A simple formula.

Courageous Calm

Change requires that that we attack it with a Courageous Calm. The dictionary defines Courage as:

"Strength in the face of adversity, grief, or pain. Pluck, valor, grit, gallantry, spunk, moxie, boldness, daring, nerve."

"I learned that courage was not the absence of fear, but the triumph over it. The brave man is not he who does not feel afraid, but he who conquers that fear."

Nelson Mandela,
Anti-Apartheid Pioneer,
President of South Africa

"He who is not courageous enough to take risks will accomplish nothing in life."

Muhammad Ali,
Boxing Champion

"You will never do anything in this world without courage. It is the greatest quality of the mind next to honor."

Aristotle

Ben embodied "Courageous Calm" in everything he attempted. He never cared what people thought of him or said about him. "Charlie, everyone is always glad to see me," Ben used to say, "Some when I ARRIVE and some when I LEAVE. But they are always glad, one way or another." He was fearless and peerless when it came to this quality. He contended it was the foremost of qualities a man could possess.

He always wanted the ball in his hands at crunch time. The state championship game, with thirty seconds to go, during the time out, he said to our high school coach, "I got this coach; give me the ball." He drove hard down the lane, kissed the ball off the glass, was hammered to the floor, and calmly drained the free throw to give us the lead. He made all fifteen of his free throws that game. I called it his "Game Face." I saw it many times after that. He had "Courageous Calm."

Are you willing to change something about you that is holding you back from manifesting your potential?

Honorable Habits

Good habits are hard to form but easy to live with. Bad habits are easy to form and hard to live with. First we form habits, then they form us.

The dictionary definition is:

"A settled or regular tendency or practice. Custom, routine, pattern, way, norm, tradition, rule or mannerism."

Your net worth to the world is usually determined by what remains after your bad habits are subtracted from your good ones. It is easier to prevent bad habits than to break them.

Ben Franklin, Author,
Inventor, Statesman, Diplomat

I never could have done what I have done without the habits of punctuality, order, and diligence, without the determination to concentrate myself on one subject at a time.

Charles Dickens, Writer, Speaker

Most people don't have that willingness to break bad habits. They have a lot of excuses and they talk like victims.

Carlos Santana, Musician, Writer

Ben was always willing to change. He adjusted his "Game" to whatever the coach needed that season. The coach asked him to play point guard his sophomore season because he grew early. He had always played the three or four position (forward) and now he was being asked to bring the ball up the court. He worked on his passing and ball handling all summer, an hour a day on the dribbling drills we learned at camp, and trying to hit an X on the wall, with both his right and left hands, a hundred times a day. He also put up a hundred free throws every day, figuring that as the point guard, in the closing minutes, he would be fouled and must be counted upon to drain the one and one. His strategy proved to be true and he sealed a lot of close games at the free-throw line. He believed in and practiced F.I.L.O. (First In, Last Out) every day for ninety days. He showed up in the fall with passing and ball handling skills no one had ever seen, and was the best free-throw shooter on the team. The price of leadership is loneliness.

What habit do you need to form? What do you need to STOP doing? What do you need to START doing?

Attitude & Altitude

There is an old expression, "Your Attitude determines your Altitude!" As cliche as that sounds, it's absolutely true. An attitude of positive expectancy and gratitude will take you further than pessimism and blame.

The dictionary definition of attitude is:

"A settled way of thinking or feeling about someone or something, typically one that is reflected in a person's behavior. Viewpoint, outlook, perspective, temper, approach, reaction, position."

Attitude is a little thing that makes a big difference.

> Attributed to Winston Churchill,
> Politician, Author, Writer

Nothing can stop the man with the right mental attitude from achieving his goal; nothing on earth can help the man with the wrong mental attitude.

> Attributed to Thomas Jefferson,
> US President, Writer, Inventor

Weakness of attitude becomes weakness of character.

> Albert Einstein, Physicist,

Ben had two predominant attitudes for as long as I knew him,

1) Expectation
2) Gratitude

He possessed a positive expectancy in all things. He knew he would win. On the rare occasion when he didn't, he would sit down and think about what he had done well and what he could have improved. He was very disciplined in that way. He also had a grateful heart, no matter what. Outwardly, his expression appeared to be just the opposite. That was when he was thinking. If you asked him what he was thinking, he would smile and say, "Well, hey, at least we are on this side of the grass," or "You know, we are young, all juniors. We will smoke those guys next year!"

How is your Attitude? How can yours be improved?

New Next

If we are not consciously changing for the better, we are unconsciously changing for the worse. We are either getting better or we are getting worse.

The dictionary definition of Next is:

"What is following in time, the next nearest in space or position. Coming immediately after the present one. Rank, upcoming, succeeding, adjacent, after, later."

"There is no better teacher than adversity. Every defeat, every heartbreak, every loss, contains its own seed, its own lesson on how to improve your performance the next time."

Malcolm X,
Author, Speaker,
Civil Rights Pioneer

"Successful people maintain a positive focus in life no matter what is going on around them. They stay focused on their past successes rather than their past failures, and on the next action steps they need to take to get them closer to the fulfillment of their goals rather than all the other distractions that life presents to them."

Jack Canfield,
Author, Speaker

"In any moment of decision, the best thing you can do is the right thing, the next best thing is the wrong thing, and the worst thing you can do is nothing."

Teddy Roosevelt,
US President, Author, Speaker

As a point guard, Ben was the coach on the floor. When I would turn the ball over and then make a stupid foul, he would holler out, "Next play!" That was his simple way of saying, "We don't have time to grieve." He understood each possession was a new start, the next play. After a setback we must look for the "New Next!"

Are you Green and Growing or Ripe and Rotting?

Giant Goals

First we work on goals, then they work on us. We become what we think about, it's the strangest secret in the world. Goals push us out of our comfort zone and force us to reach higher than we would without them.

The dictionary definition is:

"The object of a person's ambition or effort; an aim or desired result. Target, intention, desire, wish, dream, aspiration, purpose, plan."

For as long as Charlie could remember, Ben insisted they set goals. He would challenge us to think bigger than we were used to. He used to begin his sentences with, "*What if* we went undefeated this season..." or "*Imagine* when are standing at center court holding that big fat trophy over our heads as our teammates cut down the nets... how cool will that be?" Following the WHAT he would ask us about our WHYs. "What are the <u>reasons</u> we want this giant goal?"

You are never too old to set another goal or to dream a new dream.

Attributed to C.S. Lewis,
Writer, Theologian

We are at our very best, and we are happiest, when we are fully engaged in work we enjoy on the journey toward the goal we've established for ourselves. It gives meaning to our time off and comfort to our sleep. It makes everything else in life so wonderful, so worthwhile.

Earl Nightingale,
Radio Host, Speaker, Writer

Obstacles are those frightful things you see when you take your eyes off your goal.

Henry Ford, Innovator,
Father of the Automobile

Where would you like your life to be in five years? You'll be the same person in five years except for two things: the BOOKS you read and the PEOPLE with whom you associate.

Eager Edict

Someone who is eager and commands authority with his presence, attitude, charisma and able example creates followers by his sheer force of will. We follow him into battle because we believe in him.

FREEDOM FROM **FAT**

The dictionary definition is:

"An official order or proclamation issued by a person in authority. Decree, order, command, mandate, pronouncement, dictate."

> *If then true lovers have been ever crossed,*
> *It stands as an edict in destiny.*
> *Then let us teach our trial patience,*
> *Because it is a customary cross,*
> *As due to love as thoughts and dreams and sighs,*
> *Wishes and tears, poor fancy's followers.*

William Shakespeare, Poet, Playwright

> *...the great King of kings*
> *Hath in the tables of His law commanded*
> *That thou shalt do no murder. Will you then*
> *Spurn at His edict and fulfill a man's?*
> *Take heed, for He holds vengeance in His hand*
> *To hurl upon their heads that break His law.*

William Shakespeare, Poet, Playwright

Always the captain in every sport he played, the catcher and point guard, Ben would order us around, yet somehow we never seemed to mind. He did it in a way that made us want to. I have never seen anyone else do it without inciting resentment. Somehow we knew he was right and that he cared about us. He consistently gave away the credit when it was clearly his to take, and routinely accepted blame that was another's. We loved him for it. He was a true leader.

Where is this bus going? Who is on the bus? Are they in the right seats?

In a Nutshell

C.H.A.N.G.E. is an acronym. It stands for:

C = Courageous Calm

H = Honorable Habits

A = Attitude & Altitude

N = New Next

G = Giant Goals

E = Eager Edict

We are at our very best, and we are happiest, when we are fully engaged in work we enjoy on the journey toward the goal we've established for ourselves. It gives meaning to our time off and comfort to our sleep. It makes everything else in life so wonderful, so worthwhile.

In any moment of decision, the best thing you can do is the right thing, the next best thing is the wrong thing, and the worst thing you can do is nothing.

I learned that courage was not the absence of fear, but the triumph over it. The brave man is not he who does not feel afraid, but he who conquers that fear.

I never could have done what I have done without the habits of punctuality, order, and diligence, without the determination to concentrate myself on one subject at a time.

CHAPTER TWELVE

The Transformation

A giant oil painting of Ben hung in the lobby. The caption at the bottom simply said:

Benjamin Franklin Jones

1957-1994

"Whatever (It Takes)!"

It took several months for things to get back on track after Ben's passing. Most of the employees were like zombies from the movie *Night of the Living Dead*. With sadness and grief, you have to turn your rudder into the storm. You go with the flow. Crying is okay. Talking about what you miss is okay. It's normal, healthy, and healing.

Fifteen interviews to find the right person to take Ben's place as VP of Service and Operations. Steve Miles was a star. A headhunter found him in St. Charles, Missouri. It took Steve about three weeks to get up to speed, memorize every person's name, and feel accepted. Big shoes to fill. It took a lot longer to build the trust and for the comparisons to stop. It was tough for Steve to hear on a daily basis, "Ben used to..." or "That's not the way Ben did it..." Steve knew it would just take time.

Over the next three years, the company continued to grow. They attracted the best people from all over the country. There was a waiting list. They made *Inc. Magazine's* fastest-growing-companies-in-America list, and more regional awards for everything from contribution to the community to "Best Companies in the Northwest To Work For." They even received a national award, "Contractor of the Year," from *Contracting Business Magazine*.

Charlie was different after Ben's death. Gone were the fourteen-hour days. He had hired two new young Turks to bring in new business. Man, they were good. He brought in a bestselling author, speaker, and consultant from Edmonds, Washington (right in his backyard) to teach them how to sell. After two days on site, the knowledge, attitudes, skills, and habits were transferred. The young Turks hit the ground running. Charlie came in at 9:00 am and left at 4:00 pm each day. He could because the company was growing, more often than not, when he WASN'T there! Because of all the success, he was asked to speak on a regular basis: keynotes, workshops, seminars, first locally, with Kiwanis, Rotary, chambers of commerce, then, as his repute increased, with national associations, distributors, and other contractors. He only worked Monday through Wednesday; the rest of the time, when he wasn't with his family, he was on the road speaking.

One day, Charlie had his own wake up call. His physician informed him, like Ben, that he had packed on fifty pounds of excess weight. At six-foot-three he hid it well, but he knew he had to change. The defining moment came after a person in the audience came up to him after his acceptance speech for "Contractor of the Year" in Nashville, Tennessee. "Congratulations on your success! I want to introduce myself. I'm Bobby Jones, Ben's cousin." (At five-foot-nine, he looked and sounded just like Ben, save for one thing: he was at least 250 pounds!) "I'm sorry for your loss. He was a good ol' boy."

He couldn't get the image of Bobby out of his mind and it inspired him to do something physical. It had been a long time since he had worked out. That night, Charlie went back to the hotel to squeeze in a workout, perhaps a swim, and some well-deserved time in the hot tub. After his workout, he did something he had not done in a long time... he stepped onto an expensive digital scale in the hotel's weight room.

247 pounds! That could not be. He tried it again... this time sneaking up on the scale with his hand on the counter, as if that would change the outcome. 248 pounds! "What?" Charlie said aloud! "That can't be!?"

The voice of Ben echoed in his head... "Oh, it be!"

To confirm this shocking new reality, he borrowed a tape measure from the front desk to measure his waist. Forty-six inches? No... that couldn't be! He checked it again. Yep! Forty-six inches. The reality was he had become A FAT GUY IN A LITTLE COAT! A sadness came over him. Soon the sadness changed to disappointment, which quickly evolved into anger. It was the truth.

Winston Churchill said, *"The truth is incontrovertible. Panic may resent it, ignorance may deride it, malice may distort it, but there it is."*

How did this happen?

The answer was simple: inattention. He had slowly and quietly gained five pounds a year for ten years... and now it was judgment day. An accounting. The term *Inspirational Dissatisfaction* came to mind. Sick and tired of being sick and tired. By golly Charlie was going to DO something about it. He made a *DECISION!* All of this went through his head as he walked back to his hotel room. It was time for a benchmark. A starting point. He locked the door behind him, took off his shirt, looked into the mirror, and sighed. He grabbed his digital camera and took a mug shot. Two pictures, just like the police do with a man who has been arrested. He was arresting himself! He was booking the suspect. The front and side views were fingerprints. BEFORE. Two unsightly BEFORE pictures for inspiration and disgust!

He grabbed the dictionary in his briefcase and looked up the definition:

Decision (noun)

1. *The act of making up one's mind*

2. *Something that is decided, resolution*

3. *Firmness, determination, verdict*

Synonyms: Conclusion, determination, resolution, firmness, purpose, resolve, will, agreement (with one's self)

Something changed inside him. There was a shift. It was permanent. He knew it. He could feel it in his soul. The term resolve probably best described his mindset. He had a firm resolve. He thought about Ben. Would he still be alive if he hadn't been thirty to forty pounds overweight?

A phrase Charlie had used in his seminars came to mind:

"All meaningful and lasting change happens first on the inside and works its way out."

The words from mentors past and present began ringing in his ears. Twelve-step programs dealing with eating, drugs, or alcohol all over the world teach that the first three steps are: *Admitted, Believed, and Decided.* The first step to long-term change is to *admit* a problem exists. The second step is to believe change is possible. The third step is *decide* to change. All three happened that one fateful day in Boston!

In 1935, Napoleon Hill wrote, *The starting point of all achievement is desire.* He would add courage to that equation. A strong, passionate desire for something better and the courage to shoulder whatever responsibility that decision entailed. He remembered successes from his past. Once he had made a decision, the key was to follow that decision up with massive, continuous action.

The Bible, specifically the Book of James, offers a great deal about action combined with faith. It says, *Faith by itself, if it does not have works, is dead.* What does that mean? *It's simply saying; If your faith is genuine then it's going to manifest itself. There is going to be a manifestation.* Once again, he heard Ben's voice: *So, Chuck, what kind of faith have you got? I don't see any evidence!*

Charlie realized that the evidence would be the actions taken from this point forward. The next step was HONESTY. Facing the truth, the current reality as he stared at it, and it stared back at him. The truth would set him free.

Charlie grabbed his journal and wrote:

I'm Fat! My broad mind and narrow waist traded places! The current reality is that I have a stomach, a big, round, middle-aged gut! It's get-real time. I'll do this for me.

This is NOT going to be a temporary diet. DIE-it. No, this is going to be a permanent and long-term shift, a LIVE-it! It is going to be a new lifestyle. A wellness commitment.

As part of this new way of life, Charlie set some very challenging but exciting fitness goals. He would take his waist from forty-six to thirty-six inches! He would lose fifty pounds! It might take him a while, a year, maybe two. He was serious. He would get back to his playing weight in college! He wrote this new and exciting goal down on a card. He wrote and rewrote the goal in his journal. He set short, medium, and long-range goals on paper. He created both the goals and the declarations he would repeat daily.

Charlie stopped by the cemetery to visit Ben's grave, something he did regularly during the first year following Ben's passing. He would just talk to his old friend, giving him updates on the business, the family, and his own personal progress.

The engraving on Ben's tombstone always made him smile,

Ben Franklin Jones

1957-1994

"WHATEVER It Takes!"

"Well, old buddy, we are making slow but steady progress. You left a big hole to fill. I have started working out again. It feels good. The hardest part is getting to the gym, the best part is the shower afterward. I'm really going to do it—get fit, I mean—and stay that way. It would have been great to do it with you. I miss you pal."

As Charlie walked back to his car, he thought to himself, *I am doing this for myself, for my family, and I'm doing it for Ben. It will be a way for me to honor Ben's memory.* The thought brought him peace of mind. The healing had begun...

In a Nutshell

"The truth is incontrovertible. Panic may resent it, ignorance may deride it, malice may distort it, but there it is."

All meaningful and lasting change happens first on the inside and works its way out.

Admitted, Believed, and Decided.

The starting point of all achievement is desire.

Faith by itself, if it does not have works, is dead.

I'm a fat guy in a little coat! My broad mind and narrow waist traded places!

The hardest part of working out is getting to the gym, the best part is the shower afterward.

He would do this for himself, he would do it for his family, he would do it for Ben. It would be a way for him to honor Ben.

CHAPTER THIRTEEN

Fat Guy in a Little Coat

Charlie had been an athlete, a good one. He had been fit. Goals had always been a part of his life. Now he was fat. Fat guy in a little coat. He had to change. It was time for new goals.

In his seminars, Charlie taught declaring your goals aloud, five, ten, twenty, even fifty times a day. It's like programming a thermostat for a different temperature. Eventually, like the set point on the t-stat, the temperature becomes fixed. A new comfort zone. A new self-image. With that new setting comes new habits and results. It had worked in sports and grades for him as a young man. It worked for his sales and business goals. It was time to use this simple process for his wellness, for his health, for Ben's memory.

Charlie wrote his new vision on special 3 x 5 cards he had made. They said simply *"I feel alive at 195, with a 36" waist!"*

He placed the vision everywhere:

- In his bathroom on the mirror so he would see it while he shaved.

- On the dashboard of his car

- In his wallet

- On his laptop's screensaver
- In every book he read as a book mark
- On the refrigerator
- On his desk
- In his gym bag.
- In his workout journal

This was his new number-one goal. He was looking at it, saying it aloud at least twenty-five times a day... always with a smile. He imagined his new life: thin, lean, fit.

Einstein said, *"Imagination is more important than knowledge. For knowledge is limited, whereas imagination embraces the entire world, stimulating progress, giving birth to evolution."*

He broke his BIG Goal into smaller ones:

(In a month, twelve pounds and two inches off the waist): "I'm alive at 235! I enjoy a 44" waist. I love to work out."

(In three months, twenty pounds and four inches): "I feel great at 228! I enjoy a 42" waist. I am passionate about working out six times a week, every week! I am proud of ever-shrinking waistline!"

(In six months, forty pounds and eight inches): "I feel free at 203! I enjoy a 38" waist. My confidence continues to soar. I have incredible amounts of energy and vitality!"

(In twelve months, fifty-two pounds and ten inches) "I feel alive at 195 with a 36" waist!"

I eat to live, instead of living to eat!

That simple declaration, that shift in philosophy and actions would change everything. It would undo much of Charlie's past conditioning about food. Instead of eating for ego reasons, for solace, sadness, or comfort, he would simply eat to live. To nourish his body. The old aphorism *The body is a temple* made more and more sense. Not a wood-shed, a temple!

After two years of teaching other people how to change, it was time to practice what he preached on himself with his health. He listed the <u>reasons</u> he wanted to reach his goals:

- *Increased self-worth and self-respect*

- *More confidence (when I look good I feel good!)*

- *A longer and healthier life (I want to hold my great-grandson on my knee—I feel alive at 105!)*

- *His boys would be proud of him (they are athletes, he was too, once upon a time... he would be again!)*

- *When he reached his goal weight and waist, it would make a great seminar story to inspire other middle-aged men and women to change and become!*

- *Perhaps he would even turn this experience into a book. He would turn this sow's ear into a silk purse!*

In his seminars, he taught: *Road signs are the HOW that emerge when we affirm the WHAT and WHY long enough. Twenty-one to thir-ty-five days seem to be the magic number of days for the process to begin to work.* Ideas and information began to flow to him.

A six-month goal of forty pounds and eight inches off of his waist was a reasonable expectation. But could he lose fifty pounds and ten inches from his waist in one year? Getting back to his college playing weight? Now that was a challenging goal to be certain!

He began to do some research. He needed mentors. He knew from experience that if he could just talk to enough people, in this case, mid-dle aged men and women who had lost thirty, forty, even fifty pounds and *kept it off*, the answers he sought would be discovered.

He knew in his heart and head that the old excuses about metabolism and middle-aged weight gain were just that, *excuses*! *Rational-lies.*

Shakespeare said, *"To thine own self be true."* He had been an athlete in his younger days. That athlete had been *hiding in plain sight.* He would let the athlete in him out. He had indeed made a decision. He had proven to himself from his own history, he knew from past experience, that once he made up his mind, he always found the resolve to carry through. *Regret to wish; wish to want; want to will; will to what, when, and why!*

In a Nutshell

Eventually, like the set point on the t-stat, the temperature becomes fixed. A new comfort zone. A new self-image. With that new setting comes new habits and results.

I eat to live, instead of living to eat!

To get back to his college playing weight, now that was a challenging goal to be certain!

He knew in his heart and head that the old excuses about metabolism middle-aged weight gain were just that, excuses! Rational-lies.

Shakespeare said, "To thine own self be true."

Regret to wish; wish to want; want to will; will to what, when, and why!

CHAPTER FOURTEEN

Portions

Charlie gathered up ideas on wellness in the same way he had gathered critical common denominators his entire career on subjects like sales and marketing. He would become a sponge. He set about interviewing people who had done what he wanted to do, and who had been where he wanted to go. He talked to over fifty middle-aged men and women who had lost fifty pounds or more and kept it off, asking them:

1) What did you do to lose the weight and keep it off?

2) What books did you read?

3) What seminars or training did you invest in?

4) What advice would you offer to someone who wanted to get fit?

5) If you were just starting out now, what would you do differently?

In those interviews, ideas and patterns emerged. Charlie thought to himself, *Success leaves clues. What are they? One woman said she cut her portions in half and lost thirty-five pounds. An old friend told me he cut out bread and simply walked every day.* The information he needed came flying into his subconscious, planting seeds of change. *"I'll be the same person in five years but for two things, people and books..."*

He began reading everything he could find on wellness in magazines, newspapers, newsletters, and dozens of books. He grabbed his journal one rainy Sunday in Seattle, and wrote down what he had learned in the first month. He created a file. It was bulging. It was time to write.

"I have been in the shallow end of the pool for a few months now, and My Three Things emerged! I have long believed that success can be distilled down to three basic things in every endeavor:

Basketball = 1. Defense 2. Free Throws 3. Rebounds

Sales = 1. Activity 2. Pride in the Product 3. Offer a Choice of Yeses

Leadership = 1. Where is Bus Going? 2. Who is on the Bus? 3. Are they in the right seats on the Bus?"

Charlie was writing in his journal with fury and focus. The Ideas flowed.

"Wellness, too, had three things, and I will commit to them in the same way I have with all of the other successes I have enjoyed. **P.Q.E.** is the answer. So simple. Most great ideas are. *Anyone can do this!*" he mused.

The process, **P.Q.E.**, means:

1. **Portions**

2. **Quality**

3. **Exercise**

He turned these three simple strategies into sub-goals, affirmations, on index cards. Charlie knew from experience, "All meaningful and lasting change starts first on the inside and works its way out." He resolved aloud for effect: *"For the next thirty days I will commit to this formula".*

1. **Portions** = *"I cut my portions in half with every meal, putting the balance in Tupperware dishes or doggy bags to be*

eaten later. I have discipline and am mindful of how much I eat at every meal!"

2. **Quality** = *"I eat quality foods, salad instead of fries, grapes and carrots instead of a late-night sandwich. Saying no to rubbish (donuts & cookies) gets easier each day!"*

3. **Exercise** = *"I get to the gym every day, six days a week. I love to work out: walk, swim, yoga, weightlifting!"*

As Charlie observed and studied skinny people, fit people, slender people, he discovered they employed certain habitudes, behaviors to be emulated. He recalled a quote from a book on habits: "Good habits are hard to form but easy to live with; bad habits are easy to form and hard to live with." These are clearly GOOD Habits:

My Seven Portions Habits:

1) *I have learned that eating four to five small meals a day is a common denominator of skinny people.*

2) *I should be counting portions not calories. The meals need to fit into the palm of my hand, or fist of food. Forget dieting! Just use smaller plates.*

3) *I needed to eat slowly and enjoy every bite. Put my fork down three times per meal.*

4) *No more eating in front of the TV. In fact, it might be a good idea to cancel cable television altogether. Advertising on television is filled with junk-food ads. Ads promoting high-fat, low-fiber foods. The exact opposite of what I need to be eating. Life truly does imitate art. Television ads are a form of negative conditioning. At least for me, television drives me to the kitchen for unhealthy, frequent snacks of all the wrong kinds of empty calories, processed junk foods high in fat and calories and low in fiber and nutrition. Never mind the amount of time wasted on mindless programming. Late-night snacks*

are okay, provided they're raisins, carrots, frozen grapes, or apples with peanut butter.

5) *Drink a big glass of water before every meal. It will help fool my stomach into thinking that I'm full. It will move me toward the six-to-eight glasses a day I need to drink.*

6) *Take bread out of the equation. Only on Sunday (as in the prayer, "Give us this day our weekly bread.")*

7) *Absolutely NO seconds (or thirds) no matter how delicious the meal is. Push-aways! Delay that gratification.*

One article Charlie read mentioned a bestselling wellness book. In it he learned that four of the top ten killers caused by the so-called Western Diet were: obesity, cardiovascular disease, type-2 diabetes, and cancer.

The western diet is high in fat and processed foods and low in fiber and complex carbohydrates. Changing your Food Rules, a lifestyle change, can prolong your life by fifteen or twenty years. That got Charlie's attention.

In his journal, he captured some of the more memorable insights from books he was reading, people he interviewed, and overall observations:

Gathering the advice from his Study Skinny Mentors project, Charlie created "My New FOOD RULES"

Avoid foods advertised on television. Those who sell the most healthful foods, vegetables, fruits, and whole grains rarely have a national advertising budget.

Cook. Cooking for yourself is the only way to take back control of your dietary intake from the food scientists and food processors.

If you must snack, stick to dried fruits (raisins/cranberries), nuts (walnuts, almonds, pistachios, peanuts), and carrots to satisfy cravings in between meals.

Feel free to use gas-station restrooms. However, never get the fuel for your body from the same place you get the fuel for your car!

If you eat less you can afford to pay more for better foods. Do all your eating at a table, not a desk or in front of a television or driving. If you are not paying attention to what you are eating, you will invariably eat more and not realize it.

Practice portion control. Stop eating BEFORE you are full. The French and Japanese have done this for generations. Eat slowly. Pay attention. Always leave a little food on your plate.

Adopt the "S Policy"—No SNACKS, No SECONDS, No SWEETS except on days that begin with S!

Frequent local farmer's markets twice a week to purchase fruit and veggies. Support local business.

Then another whisper from Ben: *Where performance is measured, performance improves.*

He began to track the food he was eating in separate journal. The first twenty pounds came off in just 60 days. Customers, relatives, friends all began to comment, saying things like, "Wow, have you lost weight?" or "Are you working out? You look good."

This feedback simply strengthened his resolve, inspired him to keep going. Now it was time to focus on quality...

In a Nutshell

P.Q.E. was simple. Most great ideas are. Anyone can do this! It means:

1. Portions
2. Quality
3. Exercise

Avoid foods advertised on television. Those who sell the most healthful foods, vegetables, fruits, and whole grains rarely have a national advertising budget.

Cook. Cooking for yourself is the only way to take back control of your dietary intake from the food scientists and food processors.

If you must snack, stick to dried fruits (raisins/cranberries), nuts (walnuts, almonds, pistachios, peanuts), and carrots to satisfy cravings in between meals.

Feel free to use gas station restrooms. However, never get the fuel for your body from the same place you get the fuel for your car!

CHAPTER FIFTEEN

Quality

Charlie was on a mission. He hadn't been this excited about a subject since his freshman year in high school.

He developed the habit of paying attention to how fit women eat, especially his wife Katie. He noticed she always ordered her salad dressing on the side. When he asked her why, she smiled and said, "My Yoga friends taught me that. Just dip your fork in the dressing and stab the salad. Half the calories!" Women counted calories, swapped ideas and stories of what and how to eat, and what they do to stay slim. Women walk! In packs! Go to any mall, you see them in groups of five to seven at a time walking briskly. *No wonder they live longer than men,* Charlie thought to himself. He also noticed that women talk about real stuff, real fast, sometimes to complete strangers. *They don't keep it bottled up inside. They do "Walk-and-Talks!" Hmmm...*

Charlie was on a roll. He conducted extensive research into the science of SuperFoods and discovered *15 Foods That Will Add Years to Your Life and Life To Your Years.* He devoured the following foods testing them on himself. He took notes in his journal. There were fifteen specific foods he would commit to from now on. The regions, like Japan and the Baltics, where these foods were a part of the daily diet, had average life expectancies well above global norms. He was astounded at the level of energy and vitality he experienced once he made a habit of eating these SuperFoods.

The SuperFoods, in no particular order, are:

1. **Beans (Navy, Pinto, Lentil)**
2. **Blueberries**
3. **Broccoli**
4. **Oats**
5. **Oranges**
6. **Pumpkin**
7. **Salmon**
8. **Soybeans**
9. **Green Tea**
10. **Tomatoes**
11. **Turkey Breast**
12. **Nuts**
13. **Yogurt**
14. **Olives**
15. **Spinach**

He was determined to incorporate all of these into his daily intake of exceptionally nutritious foods, reminding himself to eat *small portions, three to four times a day!* The secret to using these foods wasn't strictly the ingredients themselves. The secret was how they were combined and prepared. Beans cooked in olive oil with broccoli and salmon on the side. Oatmeal with blueberries. It was the SYNERGY of combining the foods that assisted the body in fighting off cancer, diabetes, and heart disease. The medical studies proved these foods extended life, prevented disease, and provided increased energy, vitality, and wellness.

He was convinced that changing HOW he ate and WHAT he ate would yield benefits beyond simply losing weight. It was his own **Personal Peace-of-Mind-Promise.**

Everyone close to him noticed the change in his attitude and his waistline. A little more than a year from that fateful day in Nashville, early one morning, he stepped on the digital scale in his bathroom and it read 195 pounds! He had lost fifty pounds and, perhaps more importantly, ten inches off his waistline. What a glorious feeling!

Something else unfolded, a very pleasant surprise. One year into his commitment, the company had the best month they had ever had, then another and a third. He realized his wellness and his economic thermostats had both been adjusted UP. He was enjoying new set points and comfort zones in both. Was it a coincidence? He hadn't noticed at first. Old clients called, new clients appeared. Endless referrals flowed like water! He was awash in abundance. Were the two connected? Did a smaller waist and its accompanying feelings of worth and esteem foster more business?

As a reward for the hard work and discipline, he stopped by a men's clothing store at the airport and purchased an expensive thirty-six-inch brown belt. The sales clerk commented that his pants were a litte baggy. Charlie explained he had lost quite a bit of weight by working out and being mindful of what he ate. She said, "Keep up the good work. You look great."

A sense of confidence and self-worth washed over him. *She was right. He did indeed need to keep going. He was on the right track. However, even if you are on the right track, you'll get run over if you just sit there.* He looked forward to having his pants altered. Maybe it was time for a whole new wardrobe. It was a clear sign of progress, a benchmark proving that his new system worked.

He KNEW he would reach his goal of a thirty-six-inch waist, shedding the fat, and replacing it with muscle. He found he truly loved going to the gym six times a week. After fifteen to twenty minutes in the pool he felt invigorated. After forty-five minutes on the treadmill, he had energy to spare. A rigorous aerobic workout releases endorphins, triggering a relaxation response which culminates in a kind of positive high.

As he devoured books on fitness and nutrition new ideas flowed into his journal:

The average American drinks fifty gallons of soda per year! This explains the rise in childhood obesity.

What was once called 'adult onset' diabetes has become 'childhood onset' Diabetes. Sugared beverages now account for over 10% of the calories children and teenagers consume each day. They are worse than useless; they are empty and deadly. According to Kelly Brownell, director of Yale's Rudd Center for Food Policy and Obesity, 'What you want is to reverse the fact that healthy food is too expensive and fast food is too cheap. A soda tax would be a good start.'

In You're Not Sick, You're Thirsty! *Dr. F. Batmanghelidj contend that 60% of his patients are simply dehydrated. Your body often confuses dehydration with hunger. The solution? Double your water intake; drink eight to ten glasses per day! Charlie kept cases of water in his trunk and in his office. The bottles sprang up like crocus in early spring.*

At the next company meeting Charlie announced that, from that day on, there would be FREE water in the refrigerator for all employees. Moreover, the quality of snacks was going to change. The candy and soda machines were removed, replaced by fresh fruit, nuts, vegetable trays, all FREE.

Norms in a company start at the top. Organizational habits and attitudes about food were changing. Charlie was changing. And he was going to take the whole company with him...

In a Nutshell

Do a "Walk-and-Talk" every day!

Make your own Personal Peace-of-Mind Promise.

Keep up the good work. You look great.

Even if you are on the right track, you'll get run over if you just sit there.

The average American drinks fifty gallons of soda per year! This explains the rise in childhood obesity.

You're Not Sick, You're Thirsty!

CHAPTER SIXTEEN

Exercise

Drilling holes in old belts became one of Charlie's favorite activities. One day, one of his employees teased him about it. "Hey, look at
Charlie!" he called, as Charlie moved his waistband back and forth.

"Tease me all you want. I'm getting so skinny, it hurts to sit down!"

Charlie conducted a time-log study tracking how he invested his
time every fifteen minutes for a week. He was watching three to four
hours of mindless television every night. If he stopped watching TV
altogether, he would have more time for more important things like
family, friends, and working out six times a week. According to Marie
Winn, author of *The Plug-in Drug*, the average American watches
thirty hours of television a week!

Bruce Springsteen was right, 57 channels and nothing on! He
thought to himself. He promptly cancelled his cable subscription. An
occasional two-hour movie on big-screen TV was fine. It was something he could do with Katie.

Ben Franklin wrote, *"There are two ways of being happy—we may
either diminish our wants or augment our means—either will do; the
result is the same...if you are wise, you will do both at the same time..."*

Charlie knew he had to decrease his intake and increase his workouts, especially the aerobic aspect. So he started walking. He found an

old pocket calendar from 1990, the last year that he had worked out every day. He bought a little journal. He started writing down his daily aerobic activities.

October 15, walked 1.5 miles.

October 17, walked 2.0 miles.

October 19, walked 2.5 miles.

He had reached his goal. Now it was about STAYING fit. He did not want to drift back into old habits. One way to ensure that was to turn right around and help others become fit and healthy. *I can't keep it unless I give it away,* he wrote in his journal. *Teaching is the best way to learn and to keep what one learns.* His journal became a rough draft for what he knew would be a book. It was inevitable.

Slowly at first, all the right information began to appear. At first it was a trickle; then it was a flood. One glorious road sign after another. They began to appear in the forms of intuition, hunches, newspaper articles, conversations with strangers or newly found acquaintances in health clubs, in the produce section at his local organic grocery store, ideas overheard at coffee shops and social gatherings. The law of attraction is an interesting thing. Birds of a feather really do flock together. A new philosophy of living had emerged. This was a marathon, not a fifty-yard dash.

The idea of daily exercise began to appeal to him more and more. A workout partner at the gym said to him one day, *"The hardest part of a workout is simply getting to the gym. The best part of a workout is the shower afterward."*

Up until now he had needed a nap in the afternoons. He replaced the nap with a workout when he wasn't traveling. He knew the long days on the road meant that exercise was more important than ever. He would have to squeeze workouts in either early in the AM or late in the PM. Regardless, he knew he needed to make getting to the gym a priority.

One day, after a particularly challenging workout, he felt so good that he thought to himself, I have never said, *"Man I wish I hadn't worked out!"* This new lifestyle was fast becoming a positive addiction. His energy levels began to rise.

He kept reading books on wellness. He kept talking to people who worked out. He began making new friends. *Books and People.*

One Friday night, Charlie wandered into a used-book store. There on the shelf was *Body for Life: 12 Weeks to Mental and Physical Strength.* He read it during a single transatlantic flight, then he re-read it, making notes in the margins. It validated all the things he had been learning. Now he had a proven road map, a clear set of operating instructions. In ninety days, he was going to transform himself.

Another key insight bubbled to the surface. ***Negative Self-Talk.***

Negative self-talk sounded like this: ***It's raining. Do you really want to work out today?*** or, ***You deserve a break. It won't hurt to skip a day,*** or, ***You are in better shape than a lot of guys...*** and so it went. He called these "Rational-Lies!" He wrote them down in his journal. Mostly he followed Nike's advice: ***JUST DO IT!***

W.H. Murray wrote,

Until one is committed, there is hesitancy, the chance to draw back, always ineffectiveness. Concerning all acts of initiative (and creation), there is one elementary truth the ignorance of which kills countless ideas and splendid plans: that the moment one definitely commits oneself, the providence moves too. A whole stream of events issues from the decision, raising in one's favor all manner of unforeseen incidents, meetings and material assistance, which no man could have dreamt would have come his way. I learned a deep respect for one of Goethe's couplets:

> *Whatever you can do or dream you can, begin it.*
> *Boldness has genius, power and magic in it!*

All this information ended up in his workout journal. It was fast becoming a treasure trove of ideas and actions on wellness. Charlie made some more notes:

A Different Reason

I invested in some new running shoes and gradually increased aerobic commitment so that now I am now running up to four miles, four times a week. I started slow and began walking less than a mile. Success breeds success. I now have created some momentum. One day I even ran in the rain! My self-talk has started to change. I will run in the snow today. I swim two to three times a week. I do pushups and sit-ups three times a week. The athlete is back!

This is now a LIFESTYLE DECISION. My intention is NOT to "lose some weight, then gain it all back and then some!" The long-term goal has changed a little. I now have a really nice belt hanging from the full-length mirror right next to the measuring tape tailors use. I now see the goal is about the belt, NOT the weight. Waist for men, dress size for women. Muscle weighs more than fat. Embrace this new lifestyle, and enjoy a thirty-four-inch waist! If I weigh 210 pounds and enjoy a thirty-four-inch waist, that's okay. It will be muscle, not fat.

The greatest value of achieving this goal will be how it will make me feel to achieve it. The next best thing will be if I can assist others in doing this by writing about it. I don't get to keep it unless I give it away.

As each day goes by, it gets easier to eat smarter, cut down on my carbohydrate intake, work out daily. The momentum exists.

I am now starting to hear positive feedback from friends and clients. It's always a little risky to put yourself out there publicly about this kind of topic. What if I slip; what if I stop working out and go back to pizza, burgers, and fries? (It's called "Drifting.") That may happen. Right now, I don't see it. Why? I love how much more energy I have. I love how I feel about myself. Hey, I love how my clothes fit.

I love the fact my youngest son said to me, "Dad, I am proud of you. You look great!" When I get to the thirty-four-inch goal, I will write this up in much more detail in a book. I am thinking about calling it "Fabulously Fit @ 43!"

For now, the DECISION I made over fifteen months ago has changed how I feel about myself. I am about 195 pounds (lost fifty pounds) and my waist is thirty-six inches and shrinking.

The last few days in Seattle it has snowed fourteen inches. The health club is closed. Christmas food is calling: sweets, carbohydrates, and temptation. Where did I put those new running shoes? I wonder if they come with snow chains?

In one of his son's children's books he found a quote worth writing down,

> *"You have brains in your head.*
> *You have feet in your shoes.*
> *You can steer yourself*
> *any direction you choose.*
> *You're on your own. And you know what you know.*
> *And YOU are the guy who'll decide where to go."*
>
> Dr. Seuss

The thought occurred to him one day after a workout,:

> *"We don't see things as they are, we see things as we are."*

Charlie couldn't remember when he felt this good. The best was yet to come and he truly was enjoying the journey.

In a Nutshell

"Tease me all you want. I'm getting so skinny, it hurts to sit down!"

"57 channels and nothing on!"

"Until one is committed, there is hesitancy, the chance to draw back, always ineffectiveness. Concerning all acts of initiative (and creation), there is one elementary truth the ignorance of which kills countless ideas and splendid plans: that the moment one definitely commits oneself, the providence moves too. A whole stream of events issues from the decision, raising in one's favor all manner of unforeseen incidents, meetings and material assistance, which no man could have dreamt would have come his way. I learned a deep respect for one of Goethe's couplets:

> *Whatever you can do or dream you can, begin it.*
> *Boldness has genius, power and magic in it!"*

"The greatest value of achieving this goal will be how it will make me feel to achieve it."

"You have brains in your head.
You have feet in your shoes.

FREEDOM FROM **FAT**

*You can steer yourself
any direction you choose.
You're on your own. And you know what you know.
And YOU are the guy who'll decide where to go."*

CHAPTER SEVENTEEN

The Wall

As much progress as he was making, it was clear the easy weight was gone. Now the real work must begin. All of his research told him that there was a phenomenon called The Wall—that is, the place where and when most people give up. It's where the real work must begin. It separates the men from the boys, the girls from the women.

He had lost fifty pounds and eight inches off of his waist. That was encouraging. He realized that in order to reach his original goal of ten inches off of his waist, he was going to have go much deeper. He had to break through the wall. He set a new goal: He would drop another ten pounds or two inches, whichever came first, over the next ninety days.

Twelve Weeks is eighty-four days. He looked at the picture he took of himself with a forty-six-inch waist and weighing 247 pounds. A shiver went down his spine. He had been in the worst shape of his life. Fat and flabby at forty-two. What was the opposite? *Fabulously Fit at Forty-Three!*

He followed the twelve-week plan faithfully. It was a simple plan; most great plans are. As he had learned in his interviews, this plan called for reducing portions and eating small portions, the size of his fist, four times a day. It also called for lifting weights Mondays, Wednesdays, and Fridays. Tuesdays, Thursdays, and Saturdays were for aerobics.

He alternated bicycling with swimming and walking. It had to be something he LIKED to do! He started slow and built momentum and intensity with each passing week. This plan had worked for millions of other people, some much older than he. It was working for him! He drilled the fundamentals and kept it simple. P.Q.E. = Portions, Quality, Exercise.

One day at the gym, the over-forty guys asked him to play a pickup game of basketball. He was in shape! He could do it! His muscle memory allowed him to pick up where he left off after a couple of weeks of playing. He was knocking down game-winning threes! He was driving and dishing, making steals, grabbing rebounds. Sore as he was the next day, he realized he was on the right track. He was inspired to continue!

Day by day his energy increased. A brisk walk became one his favorite activities. In airports and hotels he took the stairs. Eventually he was up to five miles every other day. Most of his best ideas came to him while he walked; he carried note cards and a pen to jot them down during his long strolls through the woods and on the beach.

Nature brought out the best in him. The beach and the woods became a kind of spiritual experience. He could feel his stress levels diminish. He was much calmer. Friends, relatives, and clients noticed the change.

He measured everything. In his workout journal, he wrote down what he ate each day. He captured what he did in his workouts each day. It really is true, *Where performance is measured, performance improves.* He was getting from each day not just through it.

At the end of his eighty-four day commitment, he looked ten years younger. The feedback he received from clients and friends encouraged him to keep going. More importantly, he had the energy and physique of a twenty-five year old. The athlete in him began to emerge.

He was no longer *hiding in plain sight!*

Perhaps the biggest change was in his own self-worth, how he felt about himself. He liked the man staring back in the glass and that man liked him. It was a great feeling.

Every day, friends told him how great he looked. He simply smiled and said, "Thanks." Inside, he was darn proud. And why not? He had earned it. He knew it would add years to his life and life to his years!

In a Nutshell

He drilled the fundamentals and kept it simple. P.Q.E. = Portions, Quality, Exercise.

Lifting weights Mondays, Wednesdays, and Fridays. Tuesdays, Thursdays, and Saturdays were for aerobics.

Sore as he was the next day, he realized he was on the right track. He was inspired to continue!

Day by day his energy increased. Walking briskly became one his favorite activities.

He was no longer *hiding in plain sight!*

-Part Three-
Upward

CHAPTER EIGHTEEN

The Guy in the Glass

Charlie shared the information he had been gathering with his father.

He always respected his Dad's opinion. He would always patiently listen and, on occasion, he would offer additional insights that consistently proved useful. This was one of those situations. After reading what Charlie had written, he reached into his desk drawer and handed his son a ten-page document. "This will give you some insight into my past and the things I had to learn the hard way. Maybe it will help you and your children. It can't hurt."

*   *   *   *   *   *   *   *

In fourth grade I can remember standing on the playground wondering why my insides didn't match other kid's outsides. How come I didn't feel the way other kids looked? I had little to no confidence a great deal of the time.

I was beyond self-conscious. It was a self-esteem issue. Of course, at the time, I didn't understand this. I just knew I was different. Or so I thought.

Some of those feelings came from things going on at home. My father had a drinking problem, my parents' marriage was in danger of ending up on the rocks. My mother, God bless her, held it all together with baling wire and duct tape. The fear of abandonment and uncertainty hung over the house like a dark cloud, just waiting to dump a torrential downpour on us all. Please understand, I am NOT blaming my parents. They were doing the best they could with what they had, as most parents do. Sadly, they were living out the sins of the father (and mother). They were following the model they observed in their own childhoods.

The net effect was, for us kids, a lack of self-confidence, self-esteem, and self-respect. A cycle, if left unbroken, is handed down from generation to generation, like a ragged garment, moth-eaten, frayed and sullied.

What to do?

Awareness

It is said, "No problem can be solved at the level it was created." How true.

My father's mother was a low-bottom drunk, a binge drinker who was verbally and physically abusive. My father took to sports and spent most of his time with friends staying away from the worst kind of home environment. Is it any wonder he drank? The very thing he hated, he became. I didn't understand or know any of this. By the time I was fourteen years old, my dad had hit rock bottom. My mother issued an ultimatum, "Either give up the drink or move out." He chose the former. When I was twenty-two, my girlfriend (the woman who would eventually become my wife) made the same declaration. Like my father, I gave up John Barleycorn. It was simple, but not easy. I was homeless, carless, penniless, and jobless. That was the beginning of a powerful, positive and permanent transformation for me and a guarantee that my unborn children would not suffer from the sins of the father.

Self-Concept is a Four-Legged Chair

Self-Concept is like a four-legged chair. If one or more legs are missing we can't sit comfortably. One supports the next in a kind of positive circle of worth. It's important to understand each aspect. I will attempt to define and simplify each one, in order.

1) Self-Worth

2) Self-Respect

3) Self-Image

4) Self-Esteem

1) Self-<u>Worth</u> is the opinion you have about yourself. It's the value you place on yourself. With a positive sense of worth, you believe you are a good person who deserves good things. The opposite is equally true: You are bad person who deserves bad things. Like the soil, which is neutral, it will grow corn or nightshade in equal measure. One is healthy, the other is deadly. The soil doesn't care which one you water. It's a choice. A decision.

2) Self-<u>Respect</u> is regard for one's own standing or position. It's dignity, confidence with humility, self-awareness, a healthy pride. It's knowing you are good and wearing it well. It's being right-sized. It's learning from the past and looking forward to the future with a positive expectancy. It's being able to say, "I like myself today" and believing it. Self-Respect comes first, mutual respect follows. If I don't respect myself, how can I respect anyone else? One friend of mine calls it "Self-Love." I like that. If I don't love me, how can I love you?

3) Self-<u>Image</u> is a thermostat setting. It's how you see yourself. It's your comfort zone. Joyce Brothers said, *"A strong, positive self-image is the best possible preparation for success..."* It's formed from feedback, coaches, teachers, parents, siblings, others. Authorities in our life observe our behavior and report back to us. This solidifies how we see ourselves. It reinforces our belief about ourselves. It sets a pattern as to how we "talk to" ourselves, positive or negative. It's your self-concept, your perception of you. In junior high, it begins with grade point average. We say,

"I'm a 2.2 GPA!" with shame or regret, or "I'm a 4.0!" with great pride or humility. We have one for every aspect of our life. Money, relationships, parenting, driving, the list goes on and on. Maxwell Maltz, in his groundbreaking 1960 book, "Psycho-Cybernetics" wrote, *"The 'self image' is the key to human personality and human behavior. Change the self image and you change the personality and the behavior. Self image sets the boundaries of individual accomplishment."*

4) Self-<u>Esteem</u> is how we FEEL about ourselves. Sam Walton, the founder of Walmart, said, *"Outstanding leaders go out of their way to boost the self-esteem of their personnel. If people believe in themselves, it's amazing what they can accomplish."* Sadly, much of this begins at home, is reinforced at school and solidified at work. Self-esteem is the integrated sum of self-confidence and self-respect, a sense of personal efficacy and a sense of personal worth. Shakespeare said it all when he wrote, *To thine own self be true.*

So just what are the costs of a Low Self-Concept at work and home?

Here is the short list:

1) <u>Withholding</u>. This means withholding important information, support, ideas at crucial times out of spite. If I don't like or respect you, I will perform at a sub-standard level, sabotaging your efforts and, ironically, sadly, at the expense of my own as well.

2) <u>Resentment</u>. If you have the confidence I lack, I will harbor negative feelings toward you, over and over again. It's like drinking poison and hoping the other person will die. It's a "Lack Mentality" that cripples relationships, a negative habit that holds us back from joy and serenity.

3) <u>Gossip</u>. Smashing your furniture never makes mine look any better. It's dragging others into your private coterie of dysfunction and selfishness out of fear or envy. A house divided cannot stand. Character assassins are cowards with very low self-esteem.

4) <u>Fear</u>. Self-centered fear means "I am afraid I won't get what I want or I will lose what I have." Fear of criticism, fear of failure, fear of poverty. These are the ghosts that haunt the halls of a low self-esteem environment. Action cures fear. Honesty cuts fear in half.

5) <u>Avoidance</u>. With avoidance, sick days increase. Health-care costs soar. We are all wired the same way, we move toward pleasure and away from pain. Absence is a survival mechanism that allows us to cope with pain. Facing our pain diminishes its power over us.

So just how do we build and improve the self-concept in ourselves in others and what are the benefits? It comes in the form of *Positive Opposites*.

1) <u>Share</u>. Embrace "The Abundance Mentality" at work and at home. Give it away to keep it. Give away credit. Go out of your way to help others. It's a paradox. It defies logic. It's counter-intuitive. However, it works.

2) <u>Forgiveness</u>. Live and let live. Let go. Forgiveness doesn't change "The Haters," it changes the receivers. It takes away their power. Simple, not easy. Life is too short to be-little.

3) <u>Praise Pays</u>. Become a "Good Finder," lifting other people up. Make "Good for You!" and "Way to go!" and "Now you're cooking!" your most frequent phrases. Be happy for others' success and mean it. Good will is contagious.

4) <u>Faith</u>. It's the opposite of fear. Believe in yourself and others. Embrace a positive expectancy of the future and

an attitude of gratitude. Become "an inverse paranoid!" Believe that the world is out to help you succeed!

5) <u>Step Up</u>. Volunteer for projects. Learn to say "Yes" to requests. Ask yourself, "How can I increase my service to others today?" Go the extra mile in all things. Talk about tough issues. Find mentors and coaches to help you with challenges. Once you gain a measure of mastery, go help someone else.

A few other strategies have helped me over the years. These have come from books I have devoured and people I have met, both clients and mentors. Let's call them *The Common Denominators of Success*.

- **Capture Your W.I.N.S. in Your Journal.**

- **Start Your Day with an Inspirational Book**

- **Listen to Audiobooks While You Drive and Work Out**

- **Say "Thank You!" When Someone Gives You a Compliment.**

- **Associate With Positive People and Disassociate with Negative Ones.**

- **Able Example; Be the Change You Would Like to See in Others.**

- **Optimism Is a Learned Skill and a Philosophy**

Capture Your W.I.N.S. in Your Journal

W.I.N.S. is an acronym for **W**onderfully **I**nspirational **N**ever-ending **S**uccess!

When anything positive, inspiring, celebratory occurs, capture it on paper. You make a large sale, hit the game-winning shot, receive an award, get your name in the paper, have an article published, your son or daughter achieves something noteworthy, do not trust it to memory. A shoebox, a journal entry, a photograph. Find a place to put all those W.I.N.S.

Start Your Day with an Inspirational Book

Skip the paper, forget listening to news or watching it on TV, don't even take a shower, start your day with a book: the Bible, an inspiring biography, a bestselling self-help book, you get the idea. A pond needs fresh water to stay healthy and clean. Without it, algae turns the water green. Human beings need the same thing: fresh ideas, fresh insights, fresh inspiration. I have one entire bookshelf filled with at least 150 biographies and autobiographies of successful people. Some of them I have read three times.

Listen to Audio Books
While You Drive and Work Out
(Enroll in "Windshield University")

How many hours a week do you commute? In the early 1970s I drove from Edmonds to Tacoma (fifty-five miles in rush-hour traffic) every day for almost four years. What made it tolerable was an extraordinary audiocassette library provided by the company I worked for. Earl Nightingale, Brian Tracy, Lou Tice, Bob Moawad, Denis Waitley, Roger Dawson, Wayne Dyer, Jim Rohn. 1,200 hours a year x 20 years = 24,000 hours of audio learning, that's TWO University Degrees behind the wheel. Instead of a casket where you are ripe and rotting, make your car a university where you are green and growing!

Say "Thank You"
When Someone Gives You a Compliment

One Monday morning in March 1985, my wife said, "We are going to a seminar on self-esteem tonight. Be ready to go at 5:30 pm."

"Oh, sorry, no," I replied. "Georgetown is playing Villanova for the National NCAA Basketball Championship! You go; take good notes. We'll discuss upon your return." Pausing for effect, I continued, "Besides, I got all the self-esteem I need!"

She smiled and replied, "THAT my love, is part of the problem! Be ready to go at 5:30!" She gave me the "Sidelong Glance" for effect.

That seminar changed my life. It proves I don't know what's best for me! The instructor said something so simple I almost missed it: "When you give someone a compliment, you can calibrate their self-esteem by their response. If they smile and say "Thank you," they are healthy. If they argue, dismiss it in any way, they have a low self-esteem." My whole life I had been arguing with people, dismissing their kind words. No wonder the compliments eventually stopped. I learned it from my mother. She learned it from her grandmother. Sins of the Mother...

Associate with Positive People

My world is divided into two categories, "Anchors and Speedboats." Anchors are negative, caustic, angry, cynical, fear-full people who want to drag as many others to the bottom as they can. Speedboats are positive, kind, calm, enthusiastic, and *faith-full* people who want to pull you forward. Anchors away! Life is too short to hang around those barnacle-encrusted salty dogs. It's a choice. Walk away.

Able Example; Be the Change You Would Like to See in Others

In practicing the art of parenthood, an ounce of example is worth a ton of preachment. When we set an example of honesty, our children will be honest. When we encircle them with love, they will become loving. When we practice tolerance, they will become tolerant. When we meet life with laughter, they will develop a sense of humor. When we display genuine gratitude, they, too, will become grateful. Our children (and employees) are watching every move we make. We provide the able example, the model imperative. What we ARE shouts louder than anything we can SAY.

Optimism Is a Learned Skill and a Philosophy

Positive thinking is the notion that if you think good thoughts, things will work out well. Optimism is the feeling of thinking things will be well and be hopeful. When we take time to notice the things that go right it means we're getting a lot of little rewards throughout the day. The good life consists of deriving happiness by using your signature strengths every day in the main realms of living. The meaningful life adds one more component: using these same strengths to forward knowledge, power, or goodness. Optimistic people generally feel that good things will last a long time and will have a beneficial effect on everything they do. And they think that bad things are isolated: They won't last too long and won't affect other parts of life.

I wish I could go back to fourth grade as a playground teacher and put my arm around that nine-year-old boy, my low-esteemed self, and tell him, "Your future is so bright, it burns my eyes to look at it. You are going to be just fine. I believe in you!" It's what I did with my boys from that age until the present. It has made all the difference. It's not too late. Hug your children. Hug your employees. Hug your spouse. Tell them that you love them. Believe in them.

We are never too old for worth, an improved image, respect, and esteem. It's such a nice chair to sit on...

List Your Top Five W.I.N.S.
(Notable Accomplishments)

1. _____

2. _____

3. _____

4. _____

5. _____

"Pay attention to the Positive Feedback you get this week. When someone gives you a heartfelt and sincere compliment, just say "Thank you." It's not necessary to give them one in return. It is also okay to ask, "I'm curious, why do you say that?" In this way, you will learn the causes of your success. From there you can repeat the positive behavior. Applying this to business, taking it a step further, you can ask: "May I quote you?" and begin collecting positive feedback from clients for your website, proposals, and brochures. "When someone else blows your horn, it travels twice as far!"

Books on Self-Concept:

- *Psycho-Cybernetics*, by Maxwell Maltz

- *Release Your Brakes*, by Jim Newman

- *The Seven Spiritual Laws of Success*, by Deepak Chopra

- *The Psychology of Self-Esteem* by Nathaniel Branden

- *Learned Optimism* by Martin E.P. Seligman

- *Freedom from Fear*, by Mark Matteson

- *A Simple Choice*, by Mark Matteson

*   *   *   *   *   *   *   *

Charlie sat speechless. He understood where his "writing gene" had come from. He stood up and hugged his father.

"Thanks, Dad. With your permission, I will not only practice this but use it in my seminars and for the upcoming book."

His father just smiled and said, "More proud of you son I could not be."

In a Nutshell

"Relentless, repetitive self-talk is what changes our self-image."

Denis Waitley

"A strong, positive self-image is the best possible preparation for success."

Dr. Joyce Brothers

"The 'self image' is the key to human personality and human behavior. Change the self image and you change the personality and the behavior. Self image sets the boundaries of individual accomplishment."

Maxwell Maltz

"Outstanding leaders go out of their way to boost the self-esteem of their personnel. If people believe in themselves, it's amazing what they can accomplish."

Sam Walton

CHAPTER NINETEEN

Now It's YOUR Turn!

Ben's nephew Stanley came into Charlie's office one day. "Uncle Charlie, do you have a few minutes?"

Putting down the sales report he was reading, Charlie smiled and said, "You bet Stanley. What's going on?"

"My mom suggested I talk with you. I have packed on a few pounds, forty to be exact. Any advice on losing it?"

"Losing is one thing, keeping it off is quite another. Being forty pounds overweight at your height is not living, it's dying." Charlie surprised himself with his frank statement. "When I decided to lose the weight and keep it off, I made a decision. It was the same kind of decision I made at age eleven when I didn't make the starting lineup on my first basketball team. It's the kind of decision that's filled with emotion, disgust, anger, frustration, a kind of knowing that you are cheating yourself. I was fed up. Remember, no matter who you are or what you do, you absolutely, positively DO have the power to change!" He was on a roll. "Let's start with the 'What If' questions. Grab that pen over there and that legal pad.

1) WHAT IF you let your uncle guide you?

2) WHAT IF you had a proven plan, a simple outline for nutrition and exercise that works?

3) WHAT IF you only had to invest 5% of your day (that's forty-eight minutes out of sixteen waking hours) to reach your wellness goals?

4) WHAT IF you had more energy, turned fat into muscle, could add years to your life and life to your years?

5) WHAT IF it didn't matter if you were twenty-five, forty-five, or sixty-five years old, a man or a woman?

These are my Ten Positive Promises:

IMAGINE that you have more self-respect and self-esteem

IMAGINE that you receive, on a daily basis, more positive feedback and praise about how you looked

IMAGINE that your self-confidence improved

IMAGINE that you have three times the energy than before

IMAGINE that you make twice as much money

IMAGINE you are inspired to DO, HAVE, BECOME more

IMAGINE all of your relationships improved

IMAGINE that you decreased your chances of getting cancer, diabetes, heart disease, osteoporosis, or Alzheimer's by 60%

IMAGINE improving your sex life

IMAGINE saying yes to hiking, kayaking, skiing, basketball, yoga, swimming with no hesitation because you are fit"

Stanley was writing so fast, he never looked up.

"Are you hooked on your commitment to wellness yet?" Charlie asked.

"Yes!" Stanley replied.

"Going into this with your eyes wide open is a must. This is not a fifty-yard dash; it's a marathon, a lifetime commitment to a new and exciting philosophy. Are you ready to grow and realize your potential?"

Stanley was beaming. "Absolutely!"

"The first thing you need to do when you get home tonight is take your shirt off, grab your camera, and take a picture of yourself from two angles, front and side. Print the pictures and tape them, along with your list of goals, to your shaving mirror."

"Really?" Stanley replied. "It's that important?"

"Yes," Charlie intoned. "There is a world of difference between knowing what to do and actually doing it. Most people are 'educated derelicts,' they KNOW but they don't DO!"

Stanley's face turned serious. "I'm listening," he said.

"I'm going to ask you some personal questions. It's time for honest reflection. You see, real change always starts on the inside and works its way out.

1) Have you made the decision to change?

2) What are your reasons for making the decision?

3) When you look at yourself in the mirror, do you honestly like what you see?

4) How do you feel about yourself deep down inside?

5) Are you confident, energetic, and strong?

6) Do you often wonder if you are on the right path?

7) What are the pros and cons of continuing in the direction you are going?

8) Would you like to create a brighter future?

9) Would you like to live long enough to enjoy your grand-kids?

10) What if you didn't change anything?

"I would like you to go home and honestly answer the ten questions. Once you have done that, we can meet again to discuss your future vision, your goals. Are you willing to do *whatever it takes* to become someone else?"

"Yes!" Stanley said. He stood up and shook Charlie's hand. "I'm in!"

"I believe you are!" Charlie said with a smile.

They agree to meet once a week for twelve weeks to make certain that action would follow commitment.

In a Nutshell

"Losing the fat is one thing, keeping it off is quite another."

"Being forty pounds overweight at your height is not living, it's dying."

"Remember, no matter who you are or what you do, you absolutely, positively DO have the power to change!"

"WHAT IF you had a proven plan, a simple outline for nutrition and exercise that works?"

"WHAT IF you only had to invest 5% of your day (that's forty-eight minutes out of sixteen waking hours) to reach your wellness goals?"

"Most people are 'educated derelicts,' they KNOW but they don't DO!"

"Have you made the decision to change?"

"I'm in!"

CHAPTER TWENTY

Teaching the Process

After committing to his nephew for twelve weeks and seeing the results he achieved, and in an effort to keep what he had created, Charlie decided to conduct wellness seminars. Teaching the process to others was the secret to reinforcing and strengthening his own resolve and a way to serve his fellow man at the same time. With passion and enthusiasm, Charlie delivered his message, filled with hope and promise.

"What you do every day matters more than what you do every once in a while," he exclaimed. "What comes easy won't last. What lasts won't come easy!

"Here is a simple four-step formula for success:

D.A.S.H. is the perfect metaphor to simplify the process of change.

D = DECIDE

A = ACTION

S = STUDY

H = HONE

Decide

Something magical happens when you truly make a definite decision. You draw a line in the sand. Your life changes in that moment of courage and inspiration. It is truly a moment in time. It is YOUR decision. You own it. It's a WANT-to, not a HAVE-to! It is your personal *response-ability*. It's a highly emotionalized and convicted feeling. When you've had enough and are filled with inspirational dissatisfaction, that decision becomes your ***personal peace-of-mind promise***. Put it down on paper. In the case of wellness, what matters most is waist, size not weight. Dress size, not weight. Pick a number. HOW MUCH, BY WHEN? The power of the quantified objective. Every meaningful thing you will ever accomplish comes only after you make a decision.

With every decision comes two questions:

1) What do I need to STOP doing?

2) What do I need to START doing?

Asking

Commit to DO something every day to move toward your new vision. Massive action means understanding WHAT you need to do and going the extra mile, doing it six days a week for a month until the work becomes habitual. You need to give yourself a positive and healthy reward for doing the work, for delaying gratification. Eventually, work will become play and you'll look forward to doing it because you're getting results and positive feedback. Working out will evolve into fun. A.S.K. is an acronym for *Ask, Seek, Knock,* which comes from the Bible: Mathew 7:7: "Ask, and it will be given to you; seek, and you will find; knock and it will be opened to you." It means finding mentors who have done what you want to do and have been where you want to go. Ask yourself: What **books** should I read? What **exercises** do I need to focus on? How long should I engage in **aerobics**? What about **weights**, how many times a week? Design the questions and ask five people you admire for advice. The answers will unfold like a parachute.

Study

Read the books your new mentors suggest. One mentor said to me, 'For every one book I suggest, there are five that are not on my list. I already read the bad ones so you don't have to!' Invest in a journal and capture the key ideas from these books on paper and the ideas will take root without you even noticing. You'll experience a shift in attitude. Make time to listen to audiobooks. You can listen to twelve books a year during your daily commute!

Hone

Hone simply means keep what works and toss what doesn't. You must keep looking for and finding new ways to close the gap between HERE and THERE! You must understand that what got you HERE won't take you THERE! You must keep moving forward toward your goal. As your awareness changes, you gain experience, ideas, methods, and systems used by others, always improving our philosophy. Bad judgment > Experience > Good judgment is the learning model that will take you where you want to go. Capturing the insights in your journal will eventually produce the results you seek."

The Process

"Now it's your turn!" Charlie told his seminar audiences. "Answer every question to the best of your ability. Invest in a high-quality journal and paste these pages into it. A binder or a bound blank book will work just fine. This is the starting point in the process.

1. **On paper, make a decision to change for good. What is your wellness goal? How much, by when?**

_____

_____

_____

_____

_____

_____

2. Identify as many REASONS to change as you can think of, the more emotional the better (family reasons, spiritual reasons, proving-someone-wrong reasons). REASONS are the fuel for creating desire, the WHY of your WHAT! List a minimum of five WHYs!

_____

_____

_____

_____

_____

_____

3. Create a description of how you will LOOK, FEEL, and BE. What positive things will others be saying to you?

_____

_____

_____

_____

_____

4. Imagine. Close your eyes and imagine what it will be like to experience what you just wrote down in question #3. What will you be feeling?

_____

_____

_____

_____

5. Transform five elements of the vision from #4 into goals. Give yourself drop-dead deadlines and dates, and a way to measure them. Write them down.

_____

_____

_____

_____

_____

_____

6. Identify five barriers to manifesting your new vision.

_____

_____

_____

_____

_____

7. What are the positive opposites from #6? (i.e., *"I watch way too much TV!"* INTO *"I plan my television each week and limit it to ninety minutes every other night!"*).

_____

_____

_____

_____

_____

8. Read your new vision at least twice a day (AM & PM) with positive emotion every day for ninety days.

_____

_____

_____

_____

_____

9. Write down ideas, insights, progress, WINS (any positive feedback or success in your new journey).

_____

_____

_____

_____

_____

10. Find a work-out partner or buddy—accountability is key.

_____

_____

_____

_____

_____

11. Read the books listed below for inspiration and education for fifteen to twenty minutes every day.

_____

_____

_____

_____

_____

12. **Stick with It! There will be times that old thought patterns and habits will try to pull you back into your old life. Push through it.** *The juice is worth the squeeze!*

_____

_____

_____

_____

_____

Finish the Race

Charlie delivered his message like a Gospel-preaching panther, roaming the stage and stepping out into the audience. "There will be setbacks and adversity. Transform barriers into bridges! Strengthen your resolve by joining a gym and tracking your progress. Develop relationships with others on the same path. Birds of a feather really do flock together!"

He was on a roll. "Keep your word to yourself. I PROMISE! When you were a kid and you asked your parents if you could do something special, you would always follow up with the phrase *You PROMISE?* Take that same attitude and resolve with this new lifestyle.

"Focus on *enjoying the journey. The best is yet to come!* Age does not matter. The body is an amazing thing. It will respond to this new challenge and change in ways that are hard to envision right now.

"Much of this advice is counterintuitive. It flies in the face of things you have heard your whole life. Like 'Monitor your waist and not your weight.' Drilling holes in an old belt is a good feeling. Buying a new belt because you have to is a great feeling!"

Putting extra emphasis on his message, Charlie ended with, "Teach what you learn to someone else once you have achieved your waist and wellness goals. *You can't keep it until you give it away!*"

Suggested Reading List

- *Body for Life*, by Bill Phillips
- *Younger Next Year*, by Chris Cowley and Henry S. Lodge
- *The Ultimate Fit or Fat*, by Covert Bailey
- *The Game of Life and How to Play It*, by Florence Scovel Shinn
- *Creating Health*, by Deepak Chopra
- *Food Rules*, by Michael Pollan
- *The Healing Heart*, by Norman Cousins
- *Healthy Aging*, by Andrew Weil
- *Think and Grow Rich*, by Napoleon Hill
- *How to Win Friends and Influence People*, by Dale Carnegie
- *A Short Guide to a Long Life*, by David B. Agus
- *50 Secrets of the World's Longest Living People*, by Sally Beare
- *Live Young Forever*, by Jack LaLanne
- *It's About TIME*, by Mark Matteson

Final Thoughts on Wellness

Charlie ended his seminar by handing out a page with some rock-solid wellness advice.

To transform your body, weights will have to play a part in your new life. Find a trainer or a wellness mentor to guide and coach you.

Once you work out five to six times a week, what you eat will matter MORE than it ever did. Find a way to incorporate the fifteen SuperFoods into your diet on a daily basis.

Drink lots of water. Eight glasses a day will give you energy like never before. Your body will need more water than before. Listen to your body. It knows what it needs and it will tell you.

Eat four to five times a day, small portions of highly nutritious foods. Once a week, on your "Cheat Day," eat whatever you want. You heard me right. Go for it...hamburgers, fries, donuts. After a while, your body will eventually say, "Hey, what are doing to me? Are you nuts? Get me the right fuel fool!"

Remember: Good habits are hard to form but easy to live with. Bad habits are easy to form and hard to live with. This is a lifestyle shift. The workout habit will become a joy and sometimes the best part of your day.

Muscles grow when you are at rest. Alternate between aerobic and anaerobic activity. Weights one day, swimming or walking/ running the next. Stay with that formula. Fat will be replaced with muscle. You won't believe how you look and feel in a year! Be certain you take your BEFORE pictures! You will know when it's time to take the AFTER pictures.

Charlie closed with a story. "One of my favorite stories comes from seven-time Mr. Olympia, Arnold Schwarzenegger. He was doing a book signing in Los Angeles after he won his first title when an elderly gentleman asked him, 'I am seventy-four years old. Am I too old to lift weights?' Arnold smiled and replied, 'You are too old NOT to!' As if to justify his position, the man said, 'I don't want to become a bodybuilder or anything.' Arnold stopped signing the book and said, 'The moment you lift your first weight, you ARE a body-builder. Go for it. You'll be glad you did!'"

Charlie ended his seminar with a business-card exchange and a lively Q&A session that lasted thirty minutes.

In closing, Charlie advised, "Call any one of my fitness mentors, or anyone else in this room, anytime you feel like quitting. You never have to go it alone!

"Go for it. You will be glad you did. Remember, 'Whatever it takes!'"

In a Nutshell

D.A.S.H. is the perfect metaphor to simplify the process.

D = DECIDE

A = ACTION

S = STUDY

H = HONE

What is your "personal peace-of-mind promise?"

With every decision comes two questions:

   1) **What do I need to STOP doing?**

   2) **What do I need to START doing?**

"The moment you lift your first weight, you ARE a body-builder. Go for it. You'll be glad you did!"

"Remember, 'Whatever it takes!'"

Epilogue

Charlie was busy working on his first book when the phone rang in his study. It was Kim. "I found something you need to see, can I swing by?"

"Of course. I'll let Katie know. We can have lunch together," Charlie replied.

"She already knows," Kim said in a solemn tone.

"Okay, great. see you soon," he said.

Kim walked into Charlie's study. Books filled the shelves; they went around the room, an impressive collection by anyone's standards. Kim thought to herself, *Holy cow, there must be 5,000 books in this room!*

"Just how many books do you own Charlie?"

He laughed, "I'm not sure. I quit counting. Katie bugs me about it all the time. I made a deal with her. I would get rid of half of my books if she got rid of half of her clothes."

Kim began defending Katie when Charlie interrupted her, "What's going on? To what do I owe the pleasure of this unexpected but welcome visit, Sis?"

Kim rolled her eyes. "Well, Charles (in her sarcastic but polite voice), I finally got around to cleaning and organizing and I found this letter in Ben's home-office desk drawer. I thought you should have it."

Ben took the letter out of the envelope and read it.

To my best friend,

As you know, Charlie, I was never close to my older brother, as he was eight years older than me. Other than my parents, we never had much in common. I was a jock, he a musician. He left for the USAF when I was ten. I can count on my hand the number of "Good Times" we had. He was my brother by birth only. You, on the other hand, are my lifelong brother by choice, my adopted brother, my best friend. You always gave me credit for things you did. You were very unselfish in that way. You lifted me up when I was down. You were such a loyal friend, a blessing from God. We have accomplished so much together. It's funny, really, when it came to you and I, "One plus one didn't equal two, it equaled a thousand!" I love you brother. I have from the first day we met.

You brought out the best in me.

I know at times I came across as pessimistic and shy. It was a self-esteem, self-confidence issue. You were always so comfortable in the spotlight, and that's how it should be. You are special. The cool breeze in the stuffy room of life.

I am not sure why I am writing this. I guess I just needed to clarify a few things. Should anything ever happen to me, I just want you to know how I feel and what made me tick. So here goes.

From that day we crashed bikes, I knew somehow we were meant to be friends. There has always been an invisible thread that connected us. Some people call it "the red string of fate," others "The thread of destiny." Whatever it is, it's real. It's honest. It's forever.

From the first time I put on a catcher's mask and glove, I fell in love with sports. You pitching, me catching. As the point guard, tossing you the ball for an open look and watching you drain one jumper after another, was the most fun I ever had. Winning that state championship in high school and junior college was like a drug. Then we applied the same principles to business with equal success. We always made a great team. Opposites really do attract.

When you heard me say "Whatever..." what I really meant was, "I will do <u>whatever it takes to win!</u> I will do whatever it takes to be profitable and to serve the customer in ways no one else ever will." In sports as in business, I was always trying to keep up with you. Things came so easy to you. I always had to work twice as hard to get half your results. What I lacked in size I made up for in effort. What I lacked in natural talent I made up for with a positive attitude. Here is my point: I am so glad you are my teammate and business partner. It's been a hell of ride. I wouldn't trade it for all the tea in China. The best is yet to come.

William of Ockham was an English Franciscan friar and scholastic philosopher and theologian. He deduced the Law of Parsimony, the principle that states that among competing hypotheses that predict equally well, the one with the fewest assumptions should be selected. In other words, less is more. The simplest solution is most often the best.

If our business is to continue to succeed, we need to keep it simple. My Three-Things Formula for Great Customer Service:

1) *Go the Extra-Mile in all things. F.I.L.O. = First In, Last Out. Show up early and stay late when the job demands it. Wow the Customer with great service, especially in the little things (thank-you notes, leave it better than you found it, being gracious and kind). The customer is king.*

2) *Be a Great Teammate. An assist is better than a bucket. Empathy is walking a mile in an associate's shoes. Be loyal, thoughtful, selfless, caring, kind, and loving to one another.*

3) Attitude Is Everything. Act and the feelings will follow. Is a bird happy because he sings or does he sing because he is happy? Optimists have a better time, get along better with clients and co-workers, and usually get more done. It's a choice.

You will probably never read this. I guess I just needed to write it. I have always believed actions speak louder than words. These are the words behind my actions.

You will always be my best friend. You always brought out the best in me.

I could always be myself around you. When other people were walking out, that's when you walked in. I will never be able to thank you for bringing out the best in me. You have made this journey a joy. The next twenty years hold great promise and adventure. I can't wait brother.

Your friend,
Ben

Charlie put the letter down. The tears welled up. By now, Katie was in the room. The twins put their arms around Charlie. They said nothing. They simply helped him cry.

Breaking the silence, Kim handed Charlie one more document, written in Ben's hand...

I was never the brightest guy in the room. I don't know that I have ever had an original thought. I simply borrowed well. My heroes were regular guys. Big shots are little shots who just keep shooting! One of my heroes was another catcher, Yogi Berra. He always made me laugh. He was short and his words were always sweet. And, of course, Coach John Wooden, because he made me think.

Charlie smiled. That was just like Ben.

I have always tried to observe the things that work, principles that are timeless, and apply them to my life. But in order for me to process, I had to do it in my own words. I call it "The Art of Alternating Apothegm's" (It's a noun, meaning: A concise saying or maxim; an aphorism).

Here are my alternative favorites that I kept in my journal, a habit, by the way, that I borrowed from you. I hope you like them.

"Be quick but don't hurry"

"Don't worry about tomorrow until you get through today."

"Nobody goes there anymore, it's way too crowded!"

"It's the little details that are vital. Little things make big things happen."

"If you don't know where you are going, you might wind up someplace else."

"Things turn out best for the people who make the best of the way things turn out."

"Baseball is ninety percent mental and the other half is physical."

"Success is peace of mind which is a direct result of self-satisfaction in knowing you did your best to become the best you are capable of becoming."

"Whatever you do in life, surround yourself with smart people who'll argue with you."

"You can observe a lot by just watching."

"Success is never final, failure is never fatal. It's courage that counts."

"I never said most of the things I said."

"The most important thing in the world is family and love."

"The future ain't what it used to be."

"It isn't what you do, but how you do it."

"You should always go to other people's funerals; otherwise, they won't come to yours."

"Today is the only day. Yesterday is gone."

Finally, too many people look for happiness in all the wrong places. Happiness is an effect. The simple way to happiness is to keep your heart free of hate and resentment, your mind free of worry. Live simply, expect little, and give much, fill your life with love, scatter sunshine by smiling more, forget self, think and do for others. Do as you would be done by; do this for a month and it will become a habit, a 'Happiness Habit' that will change your life. Do 'Whatever it Takes' to live this...and happiness will come unannounced.

Charlie realized he had to put this information into some kind of permanent form, perhaps in the book he was writing. Yes. That is exactly what he would do. "I'll call it *A Tale of Two Brothers* in honor of Ben."

Charlie thanked the twins for the love, support, and ideas. Ben isn't gone. He will live on forever. Charlie would make sure of that...

The End... Or is it just the beginning?

About Mark Matteson

Mark Matteson is one of those rare professionals who can say he is a speaker, a consultant, and an author and mean it. His annual speaking commitment typically consists of forty keynotes, twenty seminars and workshops, and five to ten consulting engagements around the world with companies ranging from two million to twelve billion dollars in annual revenue. Mark also works with leading global companies and organizations like Microsoft, T-Mobile, GE, Surety Mutual Life, AFLAC, John Deere, Johnson Controls, Honeywell, York, Carrier, Conoco-Phillips, and Trane. He started his career as a speaker in 1993.

A committed writer, Mark has produced five books: *Freedom from Fear FOREVER; A Simple Choice; Wag More, Bark Even Less; It's About TIME;* and the international bestseller *Freedom from Fear* which has been translated into Japanese and French. Mark is also the author of ten popular e-books: *Presenting Like a Pro, Sales Success Strategies, Customer Service Excellence,* and *Sparking Success Vol. 1 & 2,* the best of the monthly e-newsletters that Mark has written since 2003. He writes a blog each week, tweets, and comments daily on LinkedIn.

Mark is frequently interviewed in the media, is considered a thought leader, an idea reporter, and an agent of change who teaches his clients HOW TO GET TWICE AS MUCH DONE IN HALF THE TIME. He has worked internationally in Australia, Canada, Aruba, and Turkey, in addition to 47 states in the U.S.

He resides in Edmonds, Washington with his wife of 38 years, Debbie.

Mark takes great pride in the fact he flunked high school English.

To contact Mark Matteson:

(t) 206-697-0454

Mark.EnjoyTheJourney.Matteson@Gmail.com

250 Beach Place, Suite 301, Edmonds, WA 98020

Go to **www.SparkingSuccess.net** for a monthly e-newsletter that Inspires and Educates both personally and professionally.

Enjoy the journey. The best is yet to come!